The MANUAL EXERCISE, &c.   *The* MANUAL EXERCISE *of the* FOOT GUARDS.

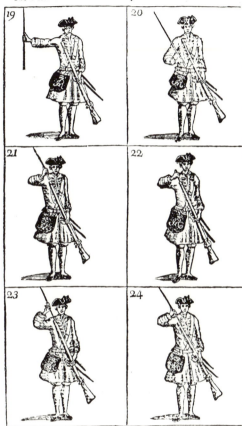

13 Cast about to charge.   14 Handle your Cartridge.   15 Open your Cartridge
16 Charge with Cartridge.   17 Draw your Rammer, *the first Motion.*   18 Draw
your Rammer, *the last Motion.*

19 Shorten your Rammer, *the first Motion.*   20 Shorten your Rammer.   21 Put
them in the Barrel.   22 Ram down your Charge.   23 Recover your Rammer
Shorten your Rammer. *See Fig.* 19.   24 Return your Rammer.

Another Part of the Field:

Philadelphia's American Revolution 1777-78

by Robert I. Alotta

Foreword by Hobart G. Cawood

WHITE MANE PUBLISHING CO., INC.
SHIPPENSBURG, PENNSYLVANIA

PICTURE CREDITS

Front and Back Endpapers; Pages 3, 16, 52, 56, 64, 68, 86, 102, 108, 114: *The American Revolution: A Picture Sourcebook.* New York, N.Y., Dover Publications, Inc., 1975.

Page 10: National Archives

Pages xiv, 20, 92, 98: Scharf, J. Thomas, and Thompson Wescott. *History of Philadelphia 1609-1884.* [4 vols.] Philadelphia: L. H. Evarts & Co., 1884.

This White Mane Publishing Company, Inc. publication
was printed by
Beidel Printing House, Inc.
63 West Burd Street
Shippensburg, PA 17257

In respect to the scholarship contained herein, the acid-free paper used in this book meets the guidelines for permanence and durability of the Committee on Production Guidelines for Book Longevity of the Council on Library Resources.

For a complete list of available publications
please write
White Mane Publishing Company, Inc.
P.O. Box 152
Shippensburg, PA 17257

Library of Congress Cataloging-in-Publication Data

Alotta, Robert I.
    Another part of the field : Philadelphia's American Revolution,
1777-78 / by Robert I. Alotta ; foreword by Hobart G. Cawood.
        p.   c.m.
    Includes bibliographical references and index.
    ISBN 0-942597-19-2 : $19.95
    1. Philadelphia (Pa.)--History--Revolution, 1775-1783.   I. Title.
F158.44.A46   1990
973.3'33--dc20
                                                                    90-21159
                                                                    CIP

PRINTED IN THE UNITED STATES OF AMERICA

To Alice...

It really doesn't make up for the lost years.

Table of Contents

Foreword

In the Delaware Valley the political events of the American Revolution are well presented at Independence National Historical Park. Some major military sites are preserved at Valley Forge National Historical Park, Brandywine Battlefield Park, Washington's Crossing State Park and Cliveden (Battle of Germantown), a property of the National Trust for Historic Preservation. Because these sites are protected and available to visitors, other important sites have been overlooked, as have many of the human interest stories that make the study of military history so exciting. Bob Alotta attempts to rectify the situation in *Another Part of the Field: Philadelphia's American Revolution 1777-78.*

What could be more heroic, exciting and historically significant than the story of Fort Mifflin? Perhaps the reason it was neglected through the years was because it was an active military post into the 1950's. Bob Alotta's effort to preserve and interpret Fort Mifflin are finally coming to pass. On July 2, 1989 the Fort was opened to the public and is being managed and restored by a private group called Fort Mifflin on the Delaware in association with the City of Philadelphia. "Hold 'to the last Extremity'" is an account of the role of Fort Mifflin and its sister Fort Mercer in the defense of the Delaware River.

Throughout this book are bits and pieces of battles, encampments, military politics, and the deeds of uncommon people. They are vignettes of the American struggle for independence and the creation of the United States of America. They can be taken one at a time, as I tend to do with my bedside reading, or in the sequence they are presented. In any case I think you will enjoy them.

Hobart G. Cawood
Superintendent
Independence National Historical Park

Introduction———

When Philadelphia Fell...

Lord William Howe, the Supreme British Commander in North America, was obsessed with the idea of capturing the most populous and most gracious city of the British colonial empire: Philadelphia.

The English commander apparently based his thinking on an old military doctrine which stated "the seizure of the capitol [when] coupled with such ascendancy over the defensive armies that they can never hope to retake it, that further resistance is felt to be hopeless, as leading only to national extinction."

During the spring of 1777, the British high command developed plans which, in their minds, would put an end to all the rebel nonsense. It was a simple strategy. General John Burgoyne would be sent down from Canada through the Lake Champlain-Hudson River route. The forces of Colonel Barry S. Leger were to sweep through the Mohawk Valley in upper New York. Howe was to move up the Hudson from New York and his brother, Admiral Richard Howe, and his fleet would seal off the eastern coast of the American continent. The combined action would isolate New England and neutralize the two main colonial ports — Philadelphia and New York. For some unknown reason, Lord Howe ignored the instructions of his superiors and deployed his forces to the south in an all-out effort against

Pennsylvania. At first he planned a naval approach to Philadelphia, but didn't leave New York with his complement of 15,000 troops until July. It was too late. Foul weather had pounded the Atlantic coast. Aboard Howe's ships, most of his horses were injured, and many of his men seasick. Rather than chance the colonial defenses in Delaware Bay, he directed his eighty ships up the Chesapeake Bay to the Head of Elk.

Why did he disregard his high command's directives? Was it to distract General George Washington's attention from the Mohawk Valley? Or might he have been looking for a warm, comfortable spot — Philadelphia — where he could weather the winter? No one knows for sure.

Washington was uncertain as to the British plans. Conflicting intelligence reports had him in turmoil. He moved his troops based on the latest rumors. Though he needed them in the Pennsylvania area, he dispatched 3,000 men to reinforce General Horatio Gates who was to hold the Hudson against Burgoyne. By August, the rumors and intelligence that the British would sail up the Chesapeake converged. Washington finally realized that Howe's objective was Philadelphia — and his attack would be overland. To stop the British force, Washington pushed his army south and lined it along Brandywine Creek at Chadd's Ford; Philadelphia to its rear, Howe in front.

Howe's first step in the Pennsylvania campaign was the Brandywine. By occupying that area, he felt he could cut off the food and provisions of the colonial army and eliminate the shops of the local gunsmiths who manufactured the lethal "Pennsylvania Rifles."

But, George Washington recognized what Howe was intending to do. Washington determined that a stand could be made at Chadd's Ford where the Philadelphia-Baltimore road forded Brandywine Creek. George Washington decided that 11 September 1777 was the time . . . and Brandywine the place . . . for the retreat of his troops to end.

On 11 September, the British attacked. Washington thought his army was facing the main British force, but he was wrong. The main army, under Howe and Lord Charles Cornwallis — and guided by former patriot, now Tory, Joseph Galloway, maneuvered itself to a ford a dozen miles north of Chadd's Ford. Unobserved, the army crossed and came down the east bank of the Brandywine and hit Washington's right flank, the flank commanded by General John Sullivan.

Through the combined efforts of Cornwallis, the Hessians, and confused, conflicting intelligence reports, the Continental Army was defeated. It was only by a brilliant rearguard action by General John Sullivan's men under Nathanael Greene and Peter Muhlenberg that the Continental Army was saved from complete destruction.

Washington moved his troops to Chester, then to Philadelphia where they picked up essential supplies and moved west toward Paoli. Washington's destination was Whitemarsh, where he hoped to regroup his army. Howe also moved east, having selected Germantown as the site for his headquarters. His baggage train, however, did not move as fast he did. It was camped near Paoli with a portion of Howe's army. General "Mad" Anthony Wayne, who lived near Paoli, convinced Washington that since he knew the area so well he could — with the assistance of 1,500 Rangers — launch a surprise attack on the British supply train and gain needed material for the Continental Army.

Moving into a secret camp, Wayne prepared to attack. But, he hadn't taken into consideration his Loyalist neighbors. They spotted Wayne's camp and reported its presence to the British. In the middle of the night, the British attacked. Removing the flints from their weapons — to prevent any premature firing which could alarm the colonials — the British attacked. The skirmish was called the "Paoli Massacre," by the colonials, but it wasn't. The Rangers suffered 400 casualties — mostly wounded. Without thinking, the men had run between the campfires and the enemy, making themselves sharp targets. Despite the swiftness and the ferocity of the attack, Wayne, though almost captured, was able to organize an orderly retreat.

At this point, it became evident that William Howe was actually intent on capturing Washington's army; Philadelphia, though attractive, was secondary in importance. He could occupy the city whenever he wanted.

At Warren's Tavern, just west of Paoli, the two armies met. It could have been a classic set-piece battle. A driving rainstorm on 16 September, however, took the battle out of human hands, rendering flintlock and cannon useless. It was, as one historian noted, "the best storm in American history, for it saved the American Army." Howe abandoned his chase of Washington after the "Battle of the Clouds" and moved into Philadelphia.

On 26 September 1777, Lord Howe entered Philadelphia. He was greeted with great warmth and ceremony by a large contingent of Philadelphians. Except for a handful of spies, the majority of patriots had fled the city, taking the Liberty Bell to Allentown and the government's files to Easton.

Though he had won the battle, Howe did not achieve the objectives for which he initially engaged in combat. He was forced to content himself only with the occupation of Philadelphia. Despite his superior force, he was unable to penetrate the heart of Pennsylvania where the farms, furnaces, forges, and supply centers for Washington's army were located. In fact, when Howe reached Philadelphia, he had to call on the remaining residents to provide 600 blankets for his troops. Firewood was in such short supply that groves of trees within the city proper were devastated; fences were taken for fuel from churches, such as St. Peter's Episcopal — a modern rector demanded restitution from the crown. And, the crowning blow to Howe: he was forced to permit the continued use of colonial currency.

Howe stabbed out from Philadelphia several times into the flexible ring with which the American general had circled the capitol city and the Schuylkill Valley, but with minor success. Though there were no battles fought while the British were ensconced in Philadelphia, there were a number of skirmishes. With all the strength they could muster, the American troops prevented the farmers and marketpeople from coming down from Bucks County to sell their wares to the British. The closest they could get was Frankford.

Washington needed a victory to encourage his men and win the popular support of the people. His intelligence network indicated that Howe had divided the British forces into two parts: a garrison under Cornwallis at Philadelphia, and about 9,000 regulars encamped near Germantown. By this time, Washington's own army had been reinforced to almost 11,000 men. So, with seemingly superior strength, the American commander decided to attack the main body of the enemy at Germantown.

The morning of 4 October 1777 greeted the advancing American army with a dense, cloying fog which reduced the troops' visibility to less than 30 yards. The superior numbers and the cover of the elements were on the side of the patriots. Victory was at hand — until something unexpected happened.

General Adam Stephen, who had been drinking heavily — to

bolster his courage — the night before, heard the sound of heavy gun-fire to his right. Without waiting for orders, Stephen wheeled his brigade about and returned the fire. "Mad" Anthony Wayne's men, hearing the sound of weaponry to their rear, feared they were sur-rounded and pulled back in panic. Blinded by fog and smoke, the two American units began shooting at each other. The result was chaotic.

George Washington took the news of his debacle philosophically. In his report to Congress, he wrote: "The enemy was nothing the bet-ter by the event; and our troops, who were not in the least dispirited by it, have gained what all young troops gain by being in actions."

Washington had been correct in his view: The American soldiers thought "they had almost won" and this bolstered their courage and resolve to fight again . . . and again . . . until victory was finally won. But before this could happen, they would have to endure the long, cold winter of 1777.

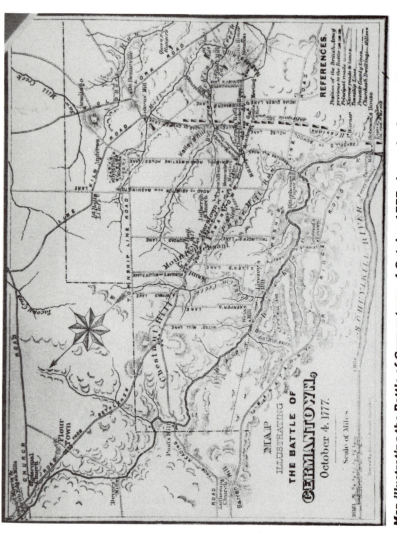

Map illustrating the Battle of Germantown, 4 October 1777, drawn by Spencer Bonsall one hundred years later.

Chapter One ─────

The Battle of Germantown: An Eyewitness Account

4 October 1777: Our army suffered defeat at the hands of the minions of the King at the small Pennsylvania community of Germantown.

Even when the tide of battle had turned against them, many participants thought victory was within the grasp of General George Washington and his troops. But a combination of the element and tactical errors tilted the balance and gained yet another success for the English.

Washington approached this battle with some fear and trepidation. Since the outset of the war, he had suffered many defeats and the Congress and the people were demanding a success.

Just recently, as everyone knows, his troops were defeated at the Brandywine. As a result, the City of Philadelphia — to the south of Germantown — collapsed into the arms of the oppressors on 26 September.

Though he had suffered loss after loss, Washington's position had suddenly become stronger — stronger than many realized.

1

The commander-in-chief had reinforced the garrisons at Forts Mifflin and Mercer on the Delaware to such a degree that the British commander, Lord William Howe, was forced to divert large numbers of his combat-ready troops to escort supplies from a safer port in Maryland into Philadelphia.

The British forces in the Philadelphia area were also divided . . . with Cornwallis in Philadelphia and the bulk — about 8,000 men — of the army encamped near Germantown.

Washington's army had been bolstered by the addition of new recruits and he could muster close to 11,000 men. Sensing the British would think him afraid to engage in battle with green troops, he decided to surprise them and attack the camp at Germantown.

With this idea in mind, Washington moved his troops five miles from their encampment near Pennypacker's Mill — about 30 miles north of Philadelphia — and set them marching down Skippack Road.

By 2 October, he was within 15 miles of Germantown. This was as close as he could safely move in daylight without giving away his position.

At a council of war, to which this reporter gained admittance, the general announced the following course of action:

He would divide his army into three parts and attack the British garrison in a simultaneous assault. They would march at night and attack at dawn.

General Nathanael Greene, of Rhode Island, would lead his three divisions — roughly two-thirds of the present army — in a wide, encircling attack down Church Lane into the British right flank. This, most reliable sources thought, would be their strongest flank.

General John Sullivan, of New Hampshire, would advance his troops right down Germantown Avenue and attack the British center.

And General William Alexander, who likes to call himself "Lord Stirling," would follow in reserve.

The key to the entire operation was to be surprise.

On 3 October, at 7 p.m., the American columns moved toward Germantown. The rough roads and the darkness hampered the men. They did not reach Chestnut Hill until dawn.

Their movement did not go undetected. As early as 3 a.m., British sentries reported seeing evidence of the American advance.

At sunrise, a dashing young Philadelphia cavalryman, Captain Allen McLane, led his light horse unit in a surprise attack on the first enemy picket post . . . near Mount Airy.

The attack was swift and thorough. McLane and his men drove the British back . . . through their camp kettles and bedding. Unfortunately, the young cavalrymen were anxious for the kill and fired their weapons prematurely. This alerted the outpost of the British 40th Regiment of Foot. That unit was able to signal the other British troops by firing its six-pound alarm gun.

McLane's men suffered no casualties and rushed back to the main body to alert General Anthony Wayne's brigade to take the lead in General Sullivan's assault down Germantown Avenue.

That morning's action will do much to enhance McLane's reputation as a darling of the young ladies of Philadelphia. As gossip has it, he courts many — if not all — of the most attractive women in the city. Prior to his commissioning as an army officer, McLane was rumored to be ready to offer marriage to young Peggy Shippen, daughter of Philadelphia's mayor.

Miss Shippen, however, married another soldier: Benedict Arnold.

When the cavalry unit returned, General Greene was not yet in position on the left. General Sullivan moved Wayne to cover that flank. Two other regiments were ordered to protect the right.

Sullivan's entire force — with Wayne in the lead — moved forward against the ranks of light infantry which had advanced to reinforce the beleaguered pickets.

Though the sun had risen, it had buried itself behind a bank of low-lying clouds. The lack of sunlight, coupled with a dense, cloying

Colonial troops attacked Cliveden, Benjamin Chew's home. The time and effort wasted by Washington's forces in attempting to take the mansion may have cost the general his chance for victory.

fog, reduced visibility to less than 30 yards. This aided the American advance, since the enemy could not see them clearly.

British Lieutenant Colonel Thomas Musgrave, commanding the 40th Regiment, formed a skirmish line across Gemantown Road. From that position, they counterattacked Sullivan's troops as they plodded through the buckwheat fields.

Musgrave's men fought fiercely. By dropping back to defend the countless fence lines that dot the area, they slowed the colonial army's progress. The British fought only when they could see the patriots; this delayed the American advance, slowing down the entire attack.

Nonetheless, the British were pushed back. But, in true English fashion, they did not acknowledge the superior strength of the patriots. In one report, we happened upon, a British officer indicated that the reason they were overrun was because "it was near the end of the campaign, [and our] battalion was very weak."

Musgrave's men were pushed back so far that the only possible place of refuge was the Chew house, set back from the corner of Germantown Avenue and Johnson Street. Finding that he and his men were surrounded, Musgrave ordered his men to occupy the place.

Chief Justice Benjamin Chew, as we all know, is an officer of the Crown. After he refused to sign a parole for the duration of the conflict, Congress ordered him and other political personages to Fredericksburg, Virginia. Since that time, his home, also known as Cliveden, has remained unoccupied, cared for only by a young couple.

Under a barrage of musket fire, Musgrave led about 120 of his men into the house, frightening the couple who were huddled under a table in the dining room.

Quickly ordering his men to barricade the doors and close the shutters, Musgrave prepared for a siege.

Sullivan, Wayne and their divisions passed the house before Musgrave's men commenced firing. It looked as though the house would be left isolated in the wake of the advancing American troops. General Henry Knox, who learned all he knows about military tactics by reading manuals in his bookstore, argued very forcibly in favor of taking the house. Despite opposition from everyone else and because of his great affection and respect for the bespectacled Knox, Washington agreed to attack.

Colonel Joseph Reed, an aide to the commander, scoffed at the notion. "Call this a fortress," he was reported to have shouted at Washington, "and lose a valuable opportunity?"

But attack they did.

"We mistook our true interest; we ought to have pushed our advantage, leaving a party to watch the enemy in that house," one American officer related to me, "but our stop here gave the enemy time to recollect themselves and get reinforced, and eventually to oblige us to retreat."

Knowing he had the building surrounded, Washington sent Lieutenant William Smith, under a flag of truce, to demand the British surrender.

Smith returned with his left leg shattered and broken by a musketball fired from the house. The cowards in the house did not recognize the white flag. Smith later died of his wounds.

Angered by this brutal and senseless murder, Washington ordered an all-out assault on the house.

Knox, who must be held responsible to some degree for the delays and casualties caused by his desire to capture the "fortress," planted four six-pound cannon on the lawn across the street — almost within musket range.

He directed his gun crews to reduce the house to rubble. But the house was — and, even after the battle, is — strongly constructed. The cannon fire was ineffective. The balls just bounced off the walls. Only one shot was true — it went through the front door and out the rear.

The patriots charged across the lawn in waves, attempting to gain entrance through the shattered door. They were driven back, suffering heavy losses by the devastating fire from the upper floors.

The lawn was littered with the bleeding and broken bodies of brave men.

The British would not — could not — be moved.

Major John White, of Sullivan's personal staff, tried to set fire to the British "castle." He raced across the lawn dodging musket fire, and reached an open window. As he prepared himself to throw his flaming missile into the room, a British Infantryman lunged through the opening and speared him with a bayonet. Major White died of the wound.

Later, another attempt was made.

Colonel John Laurens and Chevalier de Manduit Du Plessis weathered the hail of fire and lead and managed to pry open the shutters on a downstairs window. As the Frenchman was about to toss his torch into the room, a British officer rushed at him with drawn pistol. "Surrender!" he demanded. Those were his last living words. One of his privates, coming up behind him, took quick aim at Du Plessis. His aim was defective and his shot killed his own officer.

Laurens and Du Plessis, leaving the torch where it fell, ran back to the American lines, dodging bullets from both sides. Du Plessis returned unscathed but Laurens suffered a ball in his shoulder. It is uncertain which side inflicted his wound . . . but it is not serious and he will recover.

Brigadier General Francis Nash launched his North Carolina brigade in an attack on the south side of the house. A ricocheting cannonball shattered his thigh and killed his mount. Desiring more than ever to capture the British citadel, Nash disregarded his wound and shouted to his men: "Never mind me, I have had a devil of a tumble — rush on, my boys, rush on the enemy. I'll be after you presently." He never lived up to that promise. He died five days later at Whitemarsh.

Nash's aide, Major James Witherspoon, son of Dr. John Witherspoon, a signer of the congressional declaration in July of last year, was hit by the same ball. He too died.

General Adam Stephen, advancing with Greene's column, heard the raging battle in front of the Chew house — to his right — and without waiting for orders, moved his brigade out of line to join the fighting.

Greene's group, minus Stephen and his men, pushed on to hit the British right flank at the intersection of Church Lane and Limekiln Pike. Sensing that his wing was so extended that he might be outflanked, Greene veered south toward Market Square in the heart of Germantown.

General Peter Muhlenberg led his brigade in a savage bayonet attack on the British position near there. His men penetrated the enemy's front line and pushed them back for more than 1,000 yards.

But the patriots were weary from their all-night march, and their fatigue acted against them. The well-rested British troops had superior numbers in that area and they halted the advance and forced Muhlenberg to fight his way back to Greene's main body of troops.

But Colonel George Mathew, whose men had led the bayonet charge, was cut off by the British and could not retreat with the rest of Muhlenberg's force. He and his men were surrounded and captured.

Sullivan's main force was still moving down Germantown Avenue, but there was much confusion about where Greene was. Since Stephen's men had fallen in on Wayne's left, it was assumed that Greene was in position further to the left . . . and the attack was ordered as planned. Then some confused firing was heard. Shouts were heard in the distance . . . and answered from an even greater distance.

Sullivan's troops heard a loud volley of shots . . . but the return fire was sporadic and weak. Was it possible, some of the troops asked, that the enemy had moved around them? The sound of musketry got closer and more erratic.

Suddenly, men began to run out of the fog and smoke — frantic with fear. Shouts of "The enemy is in the rear . . . the flank has been turned . . . Retreat! Retreat! Retreat!" were heard. Friend had been mistaken for foe. Every man had a different story; but no one would stop long enough to have the true story deciphered.

Chaos mounted as the artillery galloped past and took the road to the rear. Officers from the front, swinging swords, cursing and pleading with their frightened men, tried to stop the panic-ridden exodus.

Washington, his staff and several mounted colonels, tried to regroup and rally the troops. They would have had more success ordering the fog to go away that day.

By 10 a.m., the panic subsided. But it was too late for Washington to do anything but order a general, orderly retreat — a retreat which, we have heard, will eventually end at Valley Forge.

Cornwallis, by this time, had come up from Philadelphia with three fresh battalions and followed Greene's men for about five miles. He did not, however, press his advantage with any determination.

The Americans had been defeated again.

The events of the day were confusing to both combatants and onlookers. Success was within the reach of the Continental forces, but because of some unknown cause or causes, the battle was lost.

Why?

From interviewing officers and enlisted men who engaged in the battle, this reporter has been able to piece together some fairly intelligent answers.

General Stephen, acting independently and without authority, collided with Wayne's troops in the fog and mistook them for the enemy. They exchanged fire and both detachments withdrew. When they learned they had been shooting at each other, they panicked and fled the field. Most informed sources state that Stephen should not have been in that position. He had not received orders to detach himself from Greene's column and was totally wrong in doing so.

It has been rumored from persons who should know that Stephen spent the night before the attack indulging to excess in alcoholic spirits to bolster his flagging courage. If this accusation proves true, Stephen should be dismissed from the army. General Washington, we have been advised, is fully aware of the reports and plans to hold a court of inquiry and take disciplinary action if necessary when the army goes into camp.

General Knox's lecturing on "castles" and "fortresses" in the rear provided the British with the opportunity to delay the advance of the entire army. In addition, it allowed the enemy to regroup its forces. The Americans, due to Knox's bookish advice, lost momentum and, as a result, were thrown into confusion.

General Greene's guide lost his way and delayed that column for more than half an hour. Greene's failure to get into proper position at the required time was yet another factor leading to the defeat. The major fault in the entire episode must rest, unfortunately, with General Washington and his plan.

The general could not expect to carry off such an innovative attack with the large number of amateur soldiers he had at his disposal. His choice of a location was ill-advised: few of his men were familiar with either the roads or the terrain . . . and he was attacking well-trained, well-disciplined professional soldiers.

This reporter was pleasantly surprised that, despite the shortcomings and the defeat, the battle came off as well as it did. As one eyewitness mentioned: "For all the misadventures, it was a near thing, a very near thing." Many thought the battle had been won, until they were told otherwise. The men, the unvictorious amateurs, do not act like they had been defeated. There is every indication that their spirits are high — higher than ever before seen in Washington's army. These green recruits look forward to another battle — as soon as possible. They have undergone a baptism of fire and none the worse for it. There losses were small but their determination is great.

It has also been learned that the French government, which has been considering whether to support the colonial cause, is suitably impressed with Washington's audacity at Germantown. It is indeed possible that they will ally themselves with us sometime in the near future. This, if it transpires, will greatly aid the American cause.

We did not win this one. But we did not lose it either. We gained more than we lost. Our shy, tender recruits gained valuable experience. They now know what war is all about — firsthand. This will serve them well in the coming months . . . until we at last are free from the yoke of royal oppression.

In an effort to reach more of an audience for history, I took it upon myself to construct an account of the Battle of Germantown for the bicentennial of the event . . . as if I were an actual eyewitness at the scene. This construct required me to do a great deal more research than I anticipated and the article, which appeared in the German-town Courier on 28 September 1977, ran much longer than any other historical newspaper article I'd written during the period . . . and longer than any the newspaper had run on any bicentennial event. Besides, I always wanted to be a war correspondent like Ernie Pyle and this was probably my only chance.

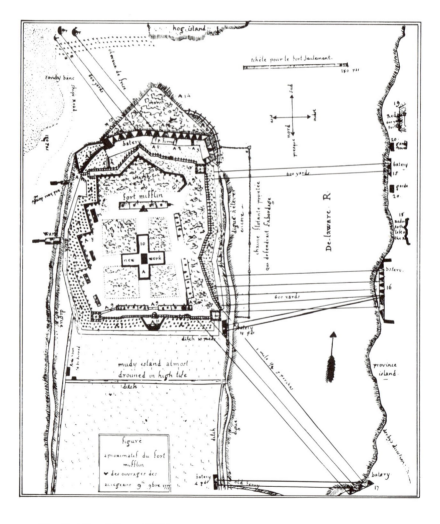

The Battle of Fort Mifflin, as seen — and drawn — by Major Fleury.

Chapter Two ————

The First Humiliation

Though warmly encamped in Philadelphia, Lord William Howe was not completely comfortable in the capital of the colonies. He needed a few things to make his life more enjoyable — such as additional supplies, ammunition, reinforcements, and rum. The fleeing colonists had taken with them a great number of items of value, and pockets of resistance kept money-hungry farmers and merchants from selling their wares in Philadelphia.

Richard Howe, admiral of the British Navy, was ordered to bring those vital supplies to his brother at the "London on the Delaware."

George Washington's intelligence reports indicated Howe was experiencing such problems and ordered the reinforcement of the two small forts on the Delaware River at Philadelphia. Properly garrisoned and fortified, these installations, Washington felt, would delay the passage of Howe's supply ships sailing up from the Delaware breakwater.

Before they left Philadelphia to the occupying enemy, the Americans "mined" the river near the confluence of the Schuylkill and Delaware Rivers with *cheveaux de frise*, reportedly devised by Benjamin Franklin. The *cheveaux* were heavy lengths of timber, tipped with iron points and set into baskets of rock. Attached to the mainland by chain, the *cheveaux* rode the waves like horses and, theoretically, would pierce the wooden hulls of any advancing ship.

Realizing what strategy the Americans had in mind, Howe made plans to attack the two river outposts — Fort Mifflin, in the middle of the Delaware, and Fort Mercer on the New Jersey side of the river at Red Bank [now National Park, N.J.]. He began bombarding the forts as early as 10 October.

"The possession of these defences is of such essential Importance to the Enemy," Washington wrote to Landon Carter, "that they are leaving no stone unturned to succeed — we are doing what we can [under many disadvantages] to disappoint them." Quietly, the commander-in-chief increased the garrison and firepower at both places. Unaware of the increased strength before them, the British forces, composed entirely of Hessian mercenaries under Colonel Carl Emil Ulrich von Donop, prepared to launch a surprise attack on the direct fortifications at Mercer.

Von Donop, relying on fragmentary information and a cursory survey, decided that the Americans could not hold the fort and would surrender if only they were asked. He had little faith in the strength of Mercer. But when he sent emissaries to the fort and asked for the surrender of the troops, he was refused.

Laughing, von Donop decided to attack. What he didn't know was that the Americans, under the directions of Polish engineer Thaddeus Kosciusczko, had altered the installation and strengthened it considerably.

When the Hessians attacked on 23 October, they discovered a newly-installed earthen wall inside what they thought were the only walls. Lacking ropes and scaling ladders, the mercenary force was stopped in its tracks. And, up to this point, not one shot had been fired.

While the Hessians stood there in utter amazement, the Americans opened fire! They poured grape and musket shot into the bunched-up, confused enemy — at point-blank range. The surprise was on the Hessians. They were massacred. Colonel von Donop never lived down the defeat. In the brief encounter, he was felled by colonial fire and died shortly after of his wounds.

Besides losing their commander, the attackers lost a full third of their men and, more important, the British suffered their first major humiliation of the Revolution. Washington was ecstatic. "The conduct of your garrison," he wrote to fellow-Virginian Robert Ballard, who fought there, "equaled my most sanguine expectations, and merits my warmest acknowledgments and thanks."

The British had to think up other ways of opening the river to their fleet. It didn't take them too long.

Garrisoned by 450 men, Fort Mifflin, the fort on Mud Island, a poorly-engineered fortification, came under British bombardment along with Mercer. Two weeks of constant bombardment and the guns at Mifflin had not been silenced. Along with supporting fire from the Pennsylvania Navy, Mifflin had inflicted severe damage on six British vessels. The 65-gun *Augusta* and the 16-gun *Merlin* were destroyed. The *Augusta* was the largest warship ever lost by Great Britain in its naval history. It was a great disgrace to a proud military tradition.

By 10 November, the British commander could stand it no longer. He decided to decimate the fort and annihilate its defenders. In what many consider the greatest artillery barrage of world history — prior to the American Civil War — one thousand cannon balls were hurled at Mifflin every 20 minutes.

Five days later, the defense had been weakened so much that British marines could fire at the American soldiers inside the fort from the riggings of the ships. Any soldier dumb enough to lift his head or peer over the walls was decapitated by the savage fire. "The garrison," Thomas Paine related, "with scarce anything to cover them but bravery, survived in the midst of mud, shot, and shells, and were at last obliged to give it up more to the powers of time and gunpowder than to military superiority of the besiegers."

The handful of survivors rowed across the Delaware to Fort Mercer on the night of 15 November . . . with the flag of the Grand Union still floating in the breeze." Cautious to the end, the British did not enter the fort until noon the next day — a good twelve hours after the firing had ceased.

The fall of Fort Mifflin was not a defeat. Obeying Washington's orders to hold the fort "to the last extremity," the small garrison provided their commander with enough time to regroup his army and march to a winter encampment.

Little has been reported in the history books about the battle of Fort Mifflin. Perhaps it is because, as Joseph Plumb Martin, a veteran of the engagement, explained: "there was not Washington, Putnam, or Wayne there . . . Great men get great praise, little men, nothing. But it always was so and always will be."

For a great part of my life — 1967-1976 — I was in-volved in the preservation and restoration of historic Old Fort Mifflin, "the last thing you see before you land at Philadelphia's International Airport." I spent over a decade studying the fort and its role in the Revolution — and

*writing about it. This particular piece, because it was writ-
ten for a newspaper, The Evening Bulletin, had to be suc-
cinct and to the point. I was able to expand more, as you
will notice, in Chapter 4. An interesting aside . . . While I
was involved at the fort, I had the opportunity to meet a
number of interesting people, including descendents of von
Donop, who were trying to do research on their ancestor's
role in the Revolution, and Lord William Howe, a descend-
ent of both the Revolution's Sir William and Philadelphia's
founder, William Penn.*

General Horatio Gates, a veteran of the French and Indian Wars, commanded the army that defeated Burgoyne at Saratoga. The purpose of the Conway Cabal was to have Gates replace Washington as the commanding general. After the cabal collapsed, Gates served in the South and suffered a disastrous defeat at Camden, South Carolina.

Chapter Three————

The Conway Cabal

George Washington's spirits were not too high as he rode to Whitemarsh, Montgomery County, Pennsylvania, with his ragged troops in the early days of November, 1777.

His mind was filled with many sobering thoughts: the defeats of his men at Brandywine and Germantown; the occupation of Philadelphia; and his own personal future.

Word had reached him that "Granny," General Horatio Gates, had been more successful than he. Gates had defeated the British at both Freeman's Farm and Bemis Heights and had accepted the surrender of 6,300 men of General "Gentleman Johnny" Burgoyne's command by terms of the Convention of Saratoga 17 October.

Though Gates' successes boosted the national morale, it caused the 45-year-old Washington to suffer a great deal of what he later called "mental discomfort." When he arrived at the Emlen House in Upper Dublin Township, where he would stay from 2 November to 11 December, Washington's thoughts were on three major issues:

He must provide better defense for the two small forts on the Delaware River. By fortifying those two installations, he would be able to harass the British and delay their fleet and keep their minds on something other than capturing the commander-in-chief and his forces.

Secondly, Washington worried about the lack of supplies — shoes, shirts, blankets, and food — for his men. As each day brought new recruits into camp, the need became more and more critical.

Finally, he was concerned about the constant internal disputes that fomented under his very nose among his cadre of senior officers. This dissension made Washington's life miserable and distracted his attention from more important things . . . like winning the war.

The key to his trouble rested mainly with one of the foreign adventurers who had joined the American army for personal gain and glory: Brigadier General Thomas Conway. Conway, a French-born Irishman, was a very ambitious man. He cultivated influential friends in Congress and elsewhere, trying to rise rapidly through the ranks . . . his eye on the post of Inspector General, which carried with it the rank of major-general.

Washington, neither a stupid man nor an isolated leader, was aware of Conway's machinations. He attempted to block the appointment by requesting the help of his old friend — and member of Congress — Richard Henry Lee. Conway's "merit, and his importance to the army," Washington wrote, "exist more in his imagination than in reality; for it is a maxim with him to leave no service of his untold, nor to want anything which is to be obtained by importunity."

Though Lee opposed Conway's nomination, other members of Congress did not. And, when news of Washington's letter reached Conway, he exploded.

Congress was not happy, to be sure, with Washington's performance and his losses in the field; and there were some congressional representatives who saw Gates as his probable successor. Knowing this, Conway began an extensive secret correspondence with the vain "Granny." He flattered the victorious commander and played up to him.

Inflated with the words of such a man — one who had highly-placed friends — Gates allowed himself to be drawn into a web of conspiracy. So enmeshed in the intrigue, Gates ignored his chain of command and withheld a direct report to his commander-in-chief regarding Saratoga.

Sensing a groundswell of support for Gates, others joined in, including Benjamin Rush, who had resigned as Surgeon General; Colonel Daniel Brodhead, of Wayne's Division; Colonel Henry E. Lutterloh, Washington's Deputy Quartermaster General; and Thomas Mifflin, who resigned as Quartermaster General to sit on the Board of War. Even John Adams, who first proposed Washington as the war commander, became involved. Together these men attacked not only George Washington, but also many of his subordinates: Generals John Sullivan, Nathanael Greene and William Alexander, the self-styled "Lord Stirling." The actions of the conspirators were undermining not only the reputation of the men involved, but also the war effort.

Through their devices, and aided by Eastern and Southern congressmen, the Board of War was reorganized and Gates placed at its head. Conway's appointment as Inspector General and his promotion to Major General were made, effective 13 December 1777. It looked as though Washington had suffered another defeat.

But luck was on his side. Colonel John Wilkinson, one of the plotters, was traveling south from Saratoga to report directly to Congress when he stopped at a tavern in Reading, Pennsylvania on 17 October. He was to meet General Mifflin there. As it happened, Lord Stirling and two of his aides were also staying at the same place. Seeing Wilkinson, the group asked him to join them for dinner and a few drinks. His tongue loosened by liquor, Wilkinson boasted that Washington was on the way out and told them about Conway's letter-writing campaign — and quoted directly: "Heaven has been determined to save your Country; or a weak General and bad Counsellors would have ruined it."

Stirling, loyal to Washington, wasted no time letting the general know what was going on behind his back. Once advised, Washington did what he had to do: he let Conway and Gates know that the cat was out of the bag and that the plot had been exposed. Both individuals assured their commander that he was mistaken. Once in the open, however, the "Conway Cabal" was over . . . and so were Conway's ambitious plans for the future. George Washington could now devote his time and energies to other priorities, like bottling up the British fleet in the Delaware River, and getting his men safely to Valley Forge and training them to fight.

It might seem strange that I would include in a patriotic package an account of an attempt by Washington's subordinates to oust him. But, a close reading of history shows that George Washington was not the dynamic leader who won battles for the colonials. At the time I wrote this piece, 8 November 1977, I felt it was important for my readers to have an idea of what some officers thought of their commander-in-chief. After rereading the account of the siege of Fort Mifflin, I could see how Washington's vacillating attitude and his painful attention to detail might have gotten on some people's nerves.

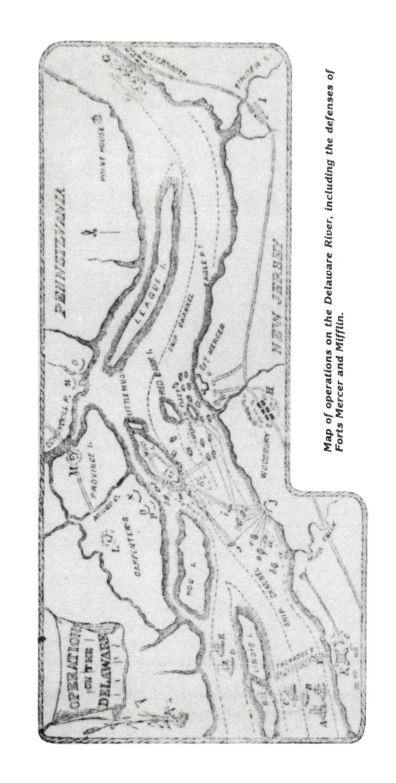

Map of operations on the Delaware River, including the defenses of Forts Mercer and Mifflin.

Chapter Four———

Hold "to the last extremity"

1771   Philadelphia was the largest city in the British colonial empire. It was also the principal seaport. To defend Philadelphia was to defend the entire colonial world. Thus, General Gage, in the spring of 1771, proposed that a British engineer stationed in New York, John Montresor, carry out the task of fortifying Philadelphia. Captain Montresor reported to Governor Richard Penn upon his arrival on 21 April. He brought with him six plans which he presented to the governor. The first of the series was a star redoubt . . . with foundations on piles. This was the beginning of the Old Fort Mifflin that exists today.

The economy-minded Board of Commissioners tried to reject the suggestion of pilings because of the great expense involved. Montresor was adamant. "A good engineer," he wrote, "is not unlike a good physician who prescribes what is most beneficial without regarding expenses. Whatever is to be done [at the fort] ought to be permanent and compleat, otherwise it will never be an honour to those that order it, nor those that execute it; on the contrary," he concluded, "[while it has an existence] it will remain an imputation of ignorance to the engineer, and of ill-tempered parsimony to the provinces.

The proposed fort, as Montesor wrote in his notebook — "Fort I built on Mud Island for the province of Pennsylvania, and for which I have never been paid, is intended to mount 32 pieces of cannon, 4 mortars, and 4 royal howitzers, making on the whole 40 pieces of ordnance, which at 6 men make 240 required, 150 musquetry, in all 400 garrison."

1772   All work on the fortifications was apparently delayed until 4 June when Montresor paced off the outline of the fort and returned to New York.

1773   The fortification, Richard Penn wrote to the engineer on 13 May, is "almost at a stand, and unable to proceed without more ample directions and some particular plan." Montresors' "personal attendance" is needed "as soon as he can make it convenient."

1774   The British never completed the Fort on Mud Island. The Provincial Assembly, on 22 January, allowed the fortifications commissioners "but just that money in Arrear to the Workmen and others concerning in Building the Fortification, should be immediately paid." The Fort On Mud Island was incapable of defending anything.

1775   Members of the Continental Congress' Committee of Safety met at Fort Island 15 October to "view the works erecting there." They felt the "men employed on Board the Boats" should have shelter, so the Committee resolved that "part of the Homes on said island be partition'd off in the middle, and that a person be employed for that purpose," and to build chimneys and fireplaces.

On 23 October, it was resolved that "Capt. Long be order'd to buy a Quantity of half Price Boards, and send them to Fort Island, for the purpose of building a leanto shed against the middle of the Fort Wall, sufficient to cover two or three hundred men in bad weather."

Thomas Proctor was appointed by the same committee on 27 October "Captain of the Company of Artillery to be raised and employed at Fort Island for the defences of this Province." Proctor was ordered to report to the Fort and take command on 9 January 1776. The Committee of Safety also voted their thanks to Captain William Davis and others who offered "their Service to act as Volunteers in the Battery to be erected at Fort Island."

The committee resolved on 30 October that Robert White and Samuel Morris be named to "a Committee to direct the building of the shed on Fort Island, . . . and to repair such buildings as may be already erected on the Island, that may be suitable to the accommodation of the soldiers and Sailors."

John Reed, along with the Messrs. Whyte and George Clymer, was appointed 19 December to report what further defenses were necessary. Reed reported to the committee that "we . . . are of the opinion that it is presently easily accessible on the West side and that there is great Danger if a Body of Men should land on that Part of the island they might surprise any Garrison posted there . . . ." To prevent this from happening, the committee wrote that "we think a proper Work might be thrown up who the Season will admit being beginning at the Waters Edge above the Southermost Bastion of the Fort now built and passing along so as to include the whole of the Fortification and the houses built on the Island that such a [line?]* with a proper Ditch and Parapet would be a great Security against any such surprise. And as any attack of this kind must from the Situation of the ground be made of Musquetry or fixed Bayonets we think a good stockaded Line would be the most proper as in that Case with a vigilant Guard and a few Men might defend it against almost any Force that could act with any Advantage on such Ground." The group further suggested "that Wolf Pits or Holes with stakes sharply pointed drove into them at suitable places would add to the security this Work is intended for."

"Upon a general view of the Island and its Communication with the mainland," the group continued, "we are of opinion that such Communication might be facilitated if a Causeway or Bank was thrown up at the nearest part of the West side of the Island to the Main Land and a good Landing place made at each shore, it appearing to this committee that in its present situation the relieving and supporting the Garrison there would be attended with much difficulty and Delay . . . ."

"With respect to the Construction of the Work first mentioned and its Form we must refer it to [someone?] skill'd in Engineering but we submit it as our opinion that Bastions will be preferable to an extended line. We would also recommend it to the Consideration of the Committee whether Guard Boats to row round the island at Night would not be very proper to prevent any surprize."

1776   The battery at the fort received an order for six 18-pound gun carriages on 24 February. On the same day, it was resolved that Captain Proctor was to have use of "as many Firelocks

---

Frequently, when I went through old documents I found watermarks or blemishes that destroyed a word or two. These I've noted with [?].

as he may have occasion for" and a 6-pound cannon. Proctor was also to "secure a flagg staff to fly the flagg of the United Colonies"; that Robert Towers would put up 50 rounds of cartridges with different kinds of shot for each of the six 18-pound cannon on the battery, and that "Mr. Owen Biddle and Captain Whyte order a Smith's Shop and Forge be erected on Fort Island, and to furnish the same with proper Smith's tools."

On 3 March, "three of the armed Boards [were] ordered down to Fort Island, and while there the men to be quartered at the Post House in rooms not occupied by Captain Proctor's Company, until sufficient barracks on Fort Island are built."

The Fort Island Committee was ordered on 16 May, at Captain Proctor's request, to have a furnace built for heating shot and to obtain "canon for [the] block house."

On 29 May, the shelter for the troops was completed . . . Captain Reed [appointed "Clerk, Commissary of Stores, and Barracks Master" at the fort 1 May] was ordered to instruct "all Boats to be stationed at Fort Island," since the barracks were "now ready for the accommodation of the officers belonging to the Boats."

On 4 July, six cannon, recently arrived from New London, were ordered sent down to the fort. Proctor was directed to "fit Carriages for them and place as many of them, for the present, on the Platform at the Battery there as it will contain."

Mid-October found Proctor a major and in need of iron stove for the barracks rooms. Reed wrote: "The Barracks are far from being close and warm as those in the City, as they are not plaster'd and many Cracks and Knot holes too plainly appear in the wether boarding . . . that the proper allowance to each Barrack may be fixt, and if possible Stoves sent down."

Proctor's men in April 1776 totaled 120; in August, they were increased to 200. On Christmas Day, part of his company was ordered to New Jersey . . . Proctor joined them and left Lieutenants Hercules Courtney and Wormsley Emes in command. By the end of the year, Major-General Thomas Mifflin was officially in charge of the work at the fort. In the same year the fort was named in his honor.

1777   Thursday, 24 July: Proctor, now a colonel, received word that he was to remove his regiment from Fort Mifflin. His men were to be replaced by a detachment from the Regiment [Corps] of Invalids — 60 men — and two Companies of Artillery [30 men each]. The garrison would be commanded by Colonel Lewis Nicola, who later would be involved in the "plot" to have Washington made king of the United States.

A letter dated 24 July, from the State Board of War to Continental Congress President Thomas Wharton, however, informed the group that Captain Hercules Courtney had alerted him that the last detachment [Third Company of Pennsylvania Artillery] of Colonel Proctor's Regiment would march that day, "in consequence of which, Fort Island will be left without a Guard."

Saturday, 26 July: Colonel Proctor wrote to Wharton: "I beg leave to inform you that the Company of Artillery under Capt'n Courtney's Command, is ordered to march for Head Quarters, to Morrow Morning . . . ."

Wednesday, 6 August: Major-General Phillippe de Coudray, an experienced French engineer, was not impressed with what he saw on a visit to the river fortification. He remarked that "The fort . . . is very bad, being inclosed, only on two fronts, by one palisade with bad loop holes, and very ill flancked."

Tuesday, 12 August: General Washington informed New Jersey's Brigadier-General Silas Newcomb that "in the interim my desire is that you order your Men to Red Bank to assist in completing the Works there [and at Fort Island]. The Officer Commanding will take orders from General de Coudray or whoever he has left there to Superintend them."

Saturday, 16 August: In view of de Coudrays' comments and suggestions — "A few chevaux de frize properly placed might effectively bar all access to the ships" — Washington recommended "but there is the possibility that any battery we can construct might be overpowered by the fire of the shipping. And as we have a few cannon and Fort Island is itself a marshy spot incapable of affording earth for the batteries necessary to be raised upon it . . . " any earth for the construction of defenses, Washington noted "must be brought from the opposite shore, it would not be prudent to multiply works there more than cannot be avoided. It would also be a great advantage gained to secure the island from annoyance, except in one point and in front from all three ships at a time, which would be effected by stopping up the passage between the two banks with chevaux de frize.

Saturday, 30 August: De Coudray returned to the fort and described it as "in a situation of being demolished in a few hours, if it be attacked in the condition in which it is at present; viz., surrounded by a single palissade, or with a wall without a terrass, which can only defend it against a coup de main, and cannot by any means resist the cannon." His advice was heeded. The fort was put into working order by the Committee of Safety, acting with the Continental Congress. In charge of the defenses were Mifflin and De Courday.

Friday, 5 September: Colonel John Bull, Adjutant-General of Pennsylvania, was instructed to report the number of men on duty in the forts on the Delaware. His report indicated "30 Continental Artillery, 15 Col. Moore's Militia and 15 Men" at Fort Mifflin.

Saturday, 6 September: The Supreme Executive Council warned Colonel Jehu [John] Eyres [Philadelphia Artillery Militia Regiment] that "The Works at Billingsport, Fort Island, Darby Creek and Bush Island, by order of his Excell'y Gen. Washington, are left almost without Guards. You will therefore immediately repair to these Works and post the two Company of Militia Artillery that are under your command, in such way as to you may appear most advantageous...."

Saturday, 13 September: Washington expressed concern about the lack of coverage at this important installation in a letter to President Wharton: "In my opinion," Washington wrote, "the River would be Sufficiently Secured against any sudden attack by Water only if the City Artillery Companies were thrown into Fort Mifflin...."

Monday, 22 September: Colonel Nicola is informed that he and his troops will be replaced by troops under the command of Colonel Henry "Baron" D'Arendt.

Tuesday, 23 September: Washington wrote D'Arendt: "I therefore appoint you to the command of [Fort Island], and desire that you will repair thither immediately. The defence is extremely interesting to the United States, and I am hopeful will be attended with much honour to yourself and advantages to them. There are Troops there now, and a Detachment to re-inforce them will immediately march from this Army."

At the same time, Washington instructed Lieutenant-Colonel Samuel Smith to "proceed with the detachment under your command to Dunk's ferry on Delaware, if you find in your progress the way clear and safe." When Smith arrived there, Washington ordered him to "take the safest and most expeditious method of conducting the detachment to Fort Mifflin; by water would be easiest and least fatiguing to your men," Washington reasoned; "and if practicable and safe, will certainly be most eligible; otherwise you will cross the Delaware and march down on the Jersey side to Fort Mifflin. In the whole march you will make all possible dispatch, keep your men in the most exact order, suffer no one to straggle, make each officer take a list of his platoon or division, and at the beginning of every march see that every man be present; you will also take every necessary precaution to prevent the enemy's surprising you on your march, by keeping out small van, flank and rear guards, and sentries when you halt . . . ."

"The keeping of the fort is of very great importance," Washington. stressed, "and I rely strongly on your prudence, spirit and bravery for a vigorous and persevering defence. The Baron Arendt will be appointed to the chief command; and when he arrives, you will give him every aid in your power."

To reinforce the fort prior to the arrival of Smith's troops, the Commander-in-Chief ordered Commodore John Hazelwood "to take out of the Ships and the Row Gallies, two or three hundred Men and Garrison the Fort with them until I can relieve them with some Continental Troops which I design as soon as possible."

Friday, 26 September: Brigadier-General John Armstrong, of the Pennsylvania Militia, affirms Washington's request in a letter to President Wharton: "The General has sent Expresses to Commodore Hazelwood to send 200 men to strengthen the Garrison of Fort Island with a French Barron to take Command of that post, wishing greatly to prevent a junction of their naval and land forces. I think he also wrote Governor of the Jersey."

Captain Enoch Anderson of the Delaware troops recounted his experience on the way to the fort: "On the seventh day from the commencement of the march of the detachment," he wrote, "I learn'd that our army had crossed over to the east bank of the Schuylkill. I inquired for the best ford on that river in that neighborhood as the late rains had raised the waters. We entered the river in platoons, — the river was about two hundred yards wide." He ordered his men "to link arm in arm, — to keep close and in compact form, and to go slow, — keeping their ranks . . . My sufferings on this tour gave myself and all of us," he recalled, "everlasting remembrance. The Germans had the advantage on us; — they were apprized of the expedition they were going on and therefore prepared to meet it. I was warned and so was all the rest of the party, to appear on grand parade as common guard for twenty-four hours; and of course was not prepared."

Saturday, 27 September: Smith's troops arrive . . . 59 men from the Maryland Regiments [1st, 2nd, 3rd, 4th, and 6th]; 56 men from the Virginia Regiments [1st, 2nd, 4th, 6th, 8th, 10th, 14th, and 16th]; 16 men from Congresses' Own [2nd Canadian]; 14 men from Colonel Walter Stewart's Pennsylvania State Regiment [the 13th];

seven men from the Delaware Regiment; three men from Colonel Pat-
ton's Additional Continental Regiment; two men from Colonel Ogden's
Regiment [the 1st New Jersey]; one man from the 4th Carolina; and
a French engineer, Major Francois Louis Teissedre de Fleury.

Colonel Smith [4th Maryland] was in command. His subordinates
included Major Robert Ballard [1st Virginia], Major Simeon Thayer [2nd
Rhode Island], Captain Samuel Treat [Company of Continental
Artillery — drawn chiefly from Colonel Lamb's Regiment] and his
lieutenant. The unit consisted of 200 infantry and a suitable company
of officers.

After seeing the condition of the Fort . . . "it was in wretched condition, without ammunition, provisions or stores, and garrisoned by
about 30 militia . . . ," Smith requested and received two additional artillery sergeants [one of whom was Moses Porter from Massachusetts,
later to advance to the rank of general during the War of 1812 — and
in command at the same installation].

Smith drew up a rough sketch of the Fort which described "a fort
walled with freestone on the side opposite to the Jersey shore" —
just as Montresor had designed years before — "and the approach
by the river; stockaded with pine logs, fifteen inches thick, opposite
Province Island; and the approach from above, flanked by three
wooded blockhouses, mounting eight-pound French guns in their upper stories. There was, also," he wote, "an open platform, on which
were mounted eighteen pounders, pointing down river, with one thirty-
two pounder, being the only piece that pointed on Province Island.

D'Arendt was reported to have been taken ill — a situation that
repeated itself frequently over the next few weeks and which posed
questions about D'Arendt's capacity to do battle. Smith assumed the
chief command.

Monday, September 29: Colonel Nicola was not made aware
of the intended date of arrival of his replacements. Thus, he planned
some reinforcements of his own. Washington wrote back to him: "I
am favoured with yours of the 25th instant from Fort Mifflin. Before
this reaches you, Lt. Col. Smith will have thrown himself into the Fort
with two hundred Continental Troops, which are all that I can possibly
spare. I very much approve of your calling upon Gov'r [William] Livingston for a Reinforcement of Jersey Militia, and I think you had better
call in the few Men that are at Billingsport and, if there are any Stores
there, remove them to Fort Mifflin."

And, almost as an afterthought, he added: "Capt'n Treat men-
tions that there is no quantity of Musket Cartridges in the Garrison,
you should immediately procure loose powder from the Ships, if you
have none in the Magazines, and set the Men to making up."

Wednesday, 1 October: Washington replied to Smith's report on the conditions at the Fort: "I am favoured with yours of the 27th Ulto. by Major [Thomas] Mullen[s] [Aide-de-Camp and Brigade-Major to General Conway] and am sorry to hear that you found matters so much out of order at Fort Mifflin . . . Two Waggon loads of Ammunition were sent from Trenton the moment Major Mullen arrived there, and I have direct Mr. [James] Mease the Clothier General to forward the necessaries wanted for your detachment." [The "necessaries" were given out to the troops on 30 September . . . so it appears Washington's directives were acted upon immediately.]

Friday, 3 October: The garrison from Billingsport retreated to Mifflin. "I ordered the People in to Boats," Colonel William Bradford wrote Washington, "and sent most of them to Fort Island."

Tuesday, 14 October: Smith was greatly concerned with the actions [or lack of] on the part of Commodore Hazelwood. He let his feelings be known to Washington, who wrote back: "In order to render the assistance of the Gallies more effectual, I am endeavoring to supply their deficiency of men from the army. In the mean time, I have desired Colonel Greene to furnish all the seamen he may have, and to give you every assistance in his power in the execution of any enterprize you may find necessary."

The conflict between the colonel and the commodore caused Hazelwood to write that the colonel "is constantly expecting the Commodore shall defend the River and at the same time defend and protect Fort Mifflin." Smith retaliated with " . . . if we had a Commodore who would do his Duty, it would be impossible for the Enemy to get Possession of this fort." [It continues to amaze me that, in the face of such a strong British threat, Smith would engage in such petty arguments.]

Wednesday, 15 October: "Col. Smith's present force," Washington wrote Colonel Christopher Greene, "is not as great as could be wished and required to be augmented, to put him in a condition to make an effectual opposition I would therefore have you detach immediately as large a part of your force as you possibly can in aid of his garrison. I cannot well determine what proportion: This must be regulated by circumstances and appearances but my present idea," the general wrote, "is that the principal part should go to his assistance. To enable you the better to spare a respectable reinforcement, I have directed Gen'l Newcomb to send his brigade of militia to Red Bank, or as many of them as he can prevail upon to go. Colonel [Israel] Angell," he informed Greene, "will also march early tomorrow morning to join you, with his regiment."

Colonel Greene [1st Rhode Island] dispatched a subaltern, a sergeant and 20 men from Fort Mercer to work at Mifflin.

Thursday, 16 October: Circumstances presented themselves in the form of intelligence as Washington wrote to Colonel Angell [2nd Rhode Island], "I think it more than probable that the greatest part of your men will be wanted in Fort Mifflin . . . ." Then Washington reported to the President of the Continental Congress: "I have therefore detached further Reinforcements to the Garrison."

Saturday, 18 October: Washington learns that D'Arendt has recovered from his "affliction." "Being recovered from the indisposition under which you lately laboured," Washington wrote to him that he was "to proceed immediately to Fort Mifflin on Mud Island and to take the command of the Troops there and those which may be sent . . . ."

"I shall not prescribe any particular line for your conduct," Washington continued, "because I repose the utmost confidence in your bravery, knowledge and judgement; and because the mode of defence must depend on a variety of circumstance, which will be best known to those, who are on the spot. I will add, that the maintenance of this post is of the last importance to the States of America, and that preventing the Enemy from obtaining possession of it, under the smiles of Heaven, will be the means of our defeating the Army to which we are opposed, or of obliging them disgracefully to abandon the City of Philadelphia, which is now in their hands . . . ."

"I have detached today a further Reinforcement to the Garrison," Washington went on, "and have instructed Col. Greene who commands at Red Bank to cooperate with you, and to render you every assistance in his power. You will maintain with him, and with Commodore Hazelwood, who commands our Fleet, a good understanding and the strictest harmony."

Then, Washington ordered Lieutenant Colonel John Green [1st Virginia Regiment] "to proceed with the Troops under your command, by the shortest Route to Bristol, where you will cross the Delaware and continue your March by way of Haddonfield to Red Bank, from whence you are to go over to Fort Mifflin, and do everything in your power for the support and defence of that garrison . . . ."

"You will take no baggage but what is absolutely necessary," Washington ordered, "and your March should be executed with the greatest secrecy and dispatch."

To be sure Red Bank knew of the advancing reinforcement, Washington alerted Colonel Greene: "Lieut. Col. Green marched this morning to reinforce the garrison at Fort Mifflin, with a detachment of two hundred Men, and Col. Arendt will immediately set out to take command of that Fort. When the Garrison was first sent to that post, this Gentleman was appointed to take command of it, but an indisposition with which he was seized prevented his entering upon it before. He is now recovered, and it devolves upon him of course . . . Col. Angell will remain with you at Red Bank and you will Cooperate with Col. Arendt, in every respect."

Sunday, 19 October: Major Simeon Thayer and a detachment of about 150 men from Angell's Regiment [3 captains, 9 subalterns, 12 sergeants, 4 drum & fifers, and 121 rank-and-file] go to Fort Mifflin to relieve a detachment of 22 men from Colonel Greene's Regiment who had been sent there earlier.

Washington's feelings on the importance of the installation were stressed in his correspondence to Hazelwood: "I am fully sensible of the importance of your station that I have sent you rather more men than were demanded for its defence, and as many of the two Rhode Island Regiments are seamen they will provide you very considerable assistance."

Monday, 20 October: Baron D'Arendt played for time. He wrote Washington that he was greatly confused with all the "greens" involved in Washington's correspondence. Washington replied with great patience . . . "Col. Christopher Greene of Rhode Island is to command at Red Bank, and Lt. Col. John Green of Virginia is to go into Fort Mifflin with the detachment under his command . . . ." And, displaying impatience for a rare moment, Washington added, "I beg you will make the greatest haste to throw yourself into Fort Mifflin . . . ."

Wednesday, 22 October: Baron D'Arendt returned to Fort Mifflin to resume command. In the face of the enemy, Fleury described him, " . . . Par Dieu! *C'est un poltron.*"

At the same time, a detachment of troops from Chandler's 8th Connecticut are moved into position to reinforce the garrison at Mifflin. A private in Captain David Smith's Company, Joseph Plumb Martin, recalled: "This day we arrived at Woodbury, New Jersey, which was the end of our present journey. We encamped near the village, planted our artillery in the road at each end of it, placed our guards and prepared to go into Fort Mifflin, on Mud Island . . . "

"Immediately after our arrival at Woodbury," Martin was ordered "upon an advanced guard, about half a mile in advance of a bridge which lay across a large creek, into which the tide flowed . . . There was a guard of the Jersey militia in advance of us."

Martin's unit was soon relieved and sent to Mifflin "to reinforce those in the fort, which was then besieged by the British. Here I endured hardships sufficient to kill half a dozen horses."

Washington wrote General Newcomb . . . again. "I must request that you do everything in your power to throw in supplies of provision to Fort Mifflin and Red Bank, this I conceive to be a matter of the utmost importance, as the Enemy may intend to starve them out."

Smith, at Fort Mifflin, was not too overjoyed with the return of D'Arendt. The Maryland native would lose his first major command. In fact, he wrote Washington of his displeasure. Washington replied: "Your Letter of 18th Inst. I received last night wherein I find you express a desire to be recalled from Fort Mifflin to join your Corps."

Thayer returned to Fort Mercer, as an advance contingent of Lieutenant-Colonel John Green's unit arrives. Smith is again displeased. Since both he and Green are lieutenant-colonels, who shall be in command? This is a question which monopolized his thinking at this critical time.

Thursday, 23 October: Washington summarized the attack on Fort Mercer in a letter to his friend Landon Carter on 27 October: "Our damage on both these occasions was inconsiderable — in the attack on Fort Mercer we had about 30 Men killed and wounded — at Fort Mifflin, and the Ships, less. The possession of these defences is of such essential Importance to the Enemy that they are leaving no stone unturned to succeed — we are doing what we can [under many disadvantages] to disappoint them."

Saturday, 25 October: The Commander-in-Chief expressed his pleasure with the repulsion of the Hessians at Fort Mercer. "I received your favour of the 23rd Inst.," he wrote Major Robert Ballard [1st Virginia] at Fort Mifflin, "and am obliged by the intelligence it contains. The conduct of your Garrison has equaled my most sanguine expectations, and merit my warmest acknowledgements and thanks."

Colonel Greene dispatched 1 captain, 3 subalterns, 4 sergeants, 2 drum & fifers, and 60 privates to reinforce the garrison at Mifflin.

25-30 October: Lieutenant-Colonel Giles Russell of Colonel John Durkee's Battalion [4th Connecticut of Varnum's Brigade] arrived with 150 men.

26 October: "You will proceed with the Detachment under your command," Washington instructed Lieutenant-Colonel Robert Ralston, "with all expedition to Red Bank, where you will receive further orders from Col. Greene, commanding officer at the Post, to which you will punctually conform."

Later the same day, Washington informed Colonel Greene that

"I have sent down Lt. Col. Ralston with three hundred Pennsylvania militia to reinforce Forts Mercer and Mifflin. I therefore desire that you and Baron Arendt will settle the proportion that each is to have, upon the most equitable terms. If you should have been joined by such a number of Jersey militia as will render your post quite secure, you are to permit all the Pennsylvania militia to pass over to Fort Mifflin."

At Fort Mifflin, D'Arendt is again taken ill. He left and Smith resumed command. Apparently D'Arendt never took actual command of the post but permitted Smith to carry on as if D'Arendt wasn't even there, which for all practical purposes he was not.

Tuesday, 28 October: Smith feared that with the arrival of Lieutenant-Colonel Green, his command would again be challenged. And, with the return of D'Arendt, he was willing to resign his post rather than have another officer assume command. Green was aware of this and stated that his commission was dated "ye 23rd of December last." Smith countered that his was dated "the 10th." Washington entered the disagreement as a mediator and wrote to Green, informing him of D'Arendt's correspondence and that "the state of his health will make it absolutely necessary for him, to withdraw himself awhile from the garrison. I am apprehensive," Washington wrote, "that, during his absence, there may arise some difficulty about the command between you and Lt. Col. Smith, as it is uncertain which of your commissions is oldest, and cannot now be easily determined. The good of the service however requires, that disputes of such a nature should be waived, and as Lt. Col. Smith had originally the command of the post, has been longer in it, and may be supposed to have more thoroughly considered every circumstance of its defence, than one who has been less time there, there are arguments with me, in the present uncertainly; respecting rank, that it should be waived in his favour. I have no doubt that they will have their full weight with you when duly considered, and that you will readily avoid any difference about punctilios, when the advancement of the service, in the last degree, may seem to require it. Relying upon this, I flatter myself," Washington wrote, "you will cheerfully acquiesce in Col. Smith's command, in the absence of the Baron, and that there will be the most perfect harmony subsisting between you."

With this knowledge — and direction — in hand, Green turns the command of his men to his second-in-command, Lieutenant-Colonel Charles Simms and withdraws.

Smith learned from Washington that the general "ordered a very handsome detachment for the reinforcements of Forts Mifflin and

Mercer, and the Gallies, they have been ready since yesterday, but the weather has been such, that they could not march. When they arrive, the duty will not be so severe, and if the men that you carried down at first can possibly be spared they shall be relieved. I will send them down necessities out of the first that arrive from Lancaster." He added . . . "I have wrote to Col. Greene to afford you every possible assistance from Red Bank till the reinforcement gets down."

Wednesday, 29 October: The Council of War learned from Washington that the garrisons at "Fort Island and Redbank; the former consisting of 300 Continental troops, the latter 350; in addition to which a detachment of three hundred militia marched the 26th. to reinforce the two posts . . ."

Thursday, 30 October: Greene sent 80 men to Mifflin, "properly officered."

Saturday, 1 November: With word of the British troop movements, Washington alerted the President of Congress: "As to Genl Newcomb, who is in the neighborhood of Red Bank, notwithstanding my most urgent and repeated solicitations, I have little to expect from him, if I may form an estimate of his future services from those he has already rendered." Newcomb's lack of response to Washington's repeated pleas culminates in the New Jersey general's resignation 4 December 1777. "Under these circumstances," Washington wrote, "I have been obliged to detach a further reinforcement of Continental Troops under Genl [James M.] Varnum to maintain the two Garrisons if possible — besides sailors drawn from the line to man the Gallies. This detachment when it arrives, added to the force now in the Forts will make the whole amount to 1600 effective rank and file sent from this Army . . ."

"The militia from Maryland and Virginia are no longer to be counted on. All the former, except about two hundred, are already gone; and a few days," the general expected, "will produce the departure of the whole or chief part of the latter from the importunate applications which some of them have made. Besides this diminution," Washington was apprehensive that "we shall have several men added to the sick list, by reason of the late excessive rain and want of clothes."

By this time, Varnum arrived at Fort Mercer. "I hope this will find you arrived safe at Red Bank with your detachment," Washington wrote. "I am afraid that matters do not go on smoothly between the Commandant at Fort Mifflin and the Commodore, as there are every now and then complaints of inattention in the Commodore; but I do not know whether with just ground."

Sunday, 2 November: Christopher Marshall in his *Remembrancer* for this date noted "... that there had been no firing on the river Since the two Ships was blown up and that Genl Washington had Sent on a Train & Company of Artillery with 300 men to reinforce the Fort at Red-bank (yesterday) that they had for Several days a most Violent Storm of wind & Rain...."

Monday, 3 November: Just as he expected, Washington told Wharton: "Agreeable to my expectation the Virginia Militia are gone, so that we have none now in aid of the Continental Troops, but those of this State mentioned in the return, and a few from Maryland. I do not know what can or will be done to obtain further reinforcements of them."

Tuesday, 4 November: "I thank you for your endeavors to restore confidence between the Commodore and Smith," Washington wrote to Varnum. "I find something of the same kind existing between Smith and Maj. Fleury, who I consider as a very valuable Officer. How strange it is that Men, engaged in the same Important Service should be eternally bickering, instead of giving mutual aid! Officers cannot act upon proper principles, who suffer trifles to interpose to create distrust and jealousy. All our actions should be regulated by one uniform Plan, and that Plan should have one object only in view, to wit, the good of the Service." [Washington's desire, though well-intentioned, was naive. Throughout the military history of the world, men worried more about their own positions and promotions than they cared about the main objectives — or why they were under arms.]

Chaplain Ebenezer David, while on a visit to Mifflin, noted: "The Commanding officer of Fort Mifflin and the Commodore are at variance (a most unhappy affaire) I forbeare to mention what has happened between them ... I could weep for the Consequences." But the bickering stopped ... either because of a reconciliation between the men brought about by Varnum or because Smith now had Fleury with whom to argue.

To quell some of the problems that Smith had with Hazelwood, Washington wrote Smith: "Enclosed is a letter to Major Fleury, whom I ordered to Fort Mifflin in quality of engineer. As he is a young man of talents, and has made this branch of military service his particular study, I place confidence in him. You will therefore make the best arrangement for enabling him to carry such plans into execution, as come within his department. His authority, at the same time that it is subordinate to yours," Washington stressed, "must be sufficient for putting into practice what his knowledge of fortifications points out as necessary for defending the post; and his department, though inferior, being of a distinct and separate nature, requires that his orders should be in a great degree discretionary, and that he should be suffered to exercise his judgement. Persuaded that you will concur with him in every measure, which the good of the service may require."

Disregarding Washington's notice, Smith used Fleury in the "capacity . . . of a grenadier." Fleury, on the other hand, had little or no regard for Smith. He said, "there are persons who know a great deal without having learnt . . . and whose obstinacy is equal to their Inefficiency." [As one can imagine, such feelings did little to enhance the cooperation that Washington wanted.]

Wednesday, 5 November: "Captn (James) Lee . . commanded the guns" in the American shore battery. He had been transferred from his post at Mifflin for this assignment.

Friday, 7 November: Preparing for the worst, Washington alerted Varnum: "No time is therefore to be lost in making that Garrison as respectable as your number will admit, for should the attack commence before they are reinforced, it may probably be out of your power to throw them in. I think," Washington concluded, "you had for the present better draw all the Continental Troops into or near Forts Mercer and Mifflin, and let what Militia are collected lay without, for I am of opinion that they will further dismay, than assist the Continental Troops, if shut up in the Forts . . ."

"As Fort Mercer cannot be attacked without considerable previous notice, I would have you spare, as many Men to Fort Mifflin as you possible can, for if accounts are to be depended upon, that is undoubtedly the post the Enemy have their designs upon."

Saturday, 8 November: Washington told General Thomas Nelson [commander of the Virginia State forces] that "they are using every effort for the reduction of Fort Mifflin and we, under our present circumstances, to save it. The event is left to Heaven."

And, then in correspondence to Varnum, "In a Letter from Genl. [Philemon] Dickinson [Major-General of the New Jersey Militia] of the 6th he informs me, that he has ordered two Detachments of Militia to march from Elizabeth Town to Red Bank, one consisting of 160 Men; he does not mention the number of the other . . ."

"I therefore repeat what I wrote Yesterday, that you should immediately reinforce Fort Mifflin as strongly as possible, and give the Commodore notice of the intended attack."

Sunday, 9 November: The enemy erected another battery on the hospital wharf on 14 October. They fired red hot shot constantly, it is reported . . . "but to little purpose, having since their first firing to the 9th November killed but two men and wounded a few, though they had thrown some thousand shot and shells."

Tuesday, 11 November: Several men, including Captain Treat, are killed. Treat and Smith were "conversing near the 32 pounder, when a ball from the enemy came. It looped in the traverse. Captain Treat tottered, and was upheld by the Colonel. A slight squeeze of the hand and he expired. No wound was apparent; and the question is, was it the sensation from the ball that caused his death?" [The manner of Treat's death was unusual, but not rare. There are several references in Revolutionary War annals to men dying from "the wind of a ball."]

Others, including the Fort's commander, were wounded. Thomas Skinner, surgeon of the 4th Connecticut, attend to Smith. Major Fleury, in his *Journal*, wrote: "*At night*. The enemy fire and interrupt our works . . . Colonel Smith, Captain George and myself wounded. These two gentlemen passed immediately to Red Bank." Major Henry, who sent daily reports of the siege to Washington, was also wounded. He, like Fleury, stayed with the garrison. The command of Fort Mifflin was then assumed by Lieutenant-Colonel Giles Russell.

Wednesday, 12 November: Unaware that Smith had been wounded and transferred to Red Bank, Washington wrote him: "I last night received your favor of the 10th instant, and am sorry to find the enemy's batteries have played with such success against our works. Nevertheless," Washington hoped "they will not oblige you to evacuate them. They are of the last importance, and I trust," Washington stressed, "will be maintained to the last extremity. I have written to General Varnum to afford you immediate succor, but sending fresh troops to relieve those now in garrison, and also such numbers of militia, as he may be able to prevail on to go to your assistance. With these, every exertion should be used for repairing in the night whatever damage the works may sustain in the day. The militia are principally designed for his end, and they are to be permitted to return every morning to Red Bank, if such should be their choice."

According to eyewitness accounts, the sound of cannon fire was deafening at Fort Mifflin . . . , so much so that Captain Cord Hazard of the Delaware Regiment was later forced to resign his commission "owing to the loss of hearing by the bursting of a shell" at Mifflin.

Washington continued to stress the importance of Mifflin. In another dispatch to Varnum, he wrote that "it is the unanimous opinion of the Council of General Officers, now sitting, that the Fort be held to the last extremity, and to enable the Commanding officer to do this, that you immediately withdraw all the invalids and fatigued men and fill up their places with the fresh and robust, and that the troops in garrison be often changed that they may by that means obtain rest . . . and therefore would have you endeavor to prevail upon the Militia to go over at night, when there is cessation of firing and work till day light. You may give them the most positive assurances that it is not meant to keep them there against their consent. This would greatly relieve the Continental Troops, and by these means a great deal of work might be done."

Four hours later, Washington wrote back to Varnum: "Since I wrote you at one OClock this day yours date twelve last Night came to hand. This has occasioned an alteration in the sentiments of myself and the council who find it impossible, from your representation, to give timely relief to the Fort. We therefore are now of opinion," he continued, "that the Cannon and Stores ought immediately to be removed and everything put into a disposition to remove totally at a minute's warning; but as every day that we can hold even the Island, is so much time gained, I would recommend a party to be left, who might find good Shelter behind Works, and when they abandon, they should set fire to the Barracks and all remaining buildings. If this was done upon a flood time, the Enemy could not come out of Schuylkill with Boats to put the fire out, or to intercept the passage of the Garrison. If what works remain could be blown up, or other-ways effectually destroyed before evacuation, it would take the Enemy so much more time and labour to make a lodgement upon the Island . . . ."

Finally aware that Smith had left the fort, Washington asked Var-num "to communicate this to Col. Smith and let him know I received his of Yesterday. I hope his wound is not dangerous."

12-13 November: Major Thayer left Fort Mercer with "100 fresh troops" to replace "the most fatigued . . . wounded" at Mifflin. Thayer also relieved Russell of command.

Colonel Angell later reflected that Thayer assumed the com-mand "by the particular request of General Varnum, unexpected as his desire was." Thayer "went over and relieved Col. Russell, and the Remainder of Col. Smith's men; part having been relieved before, with a Detachment from Col. Durkee's [4th Connecticut] and Col. [John] Chandler's [8th Connecticut] Regiments, of Genl Varnum's brigade. The garrison then consisted of 286 Rank and file, and Capt. Lee's Company of artillery of about 20 men." About 150 of these men were from Varnum's brigades.

In his memoirs, Private Joseph Plumb Martin remembered: "In the cold month of November, without provisions, without clothing, not a scrap of either shoes or stockings to my feet or legs, and in this condition to endure a siege in such a place as that was appalling in the highest degree.

"Neither this house [the officer's] nor the barracks were of much use at this time, for it was as much as a man's life was worth to enter them, the enemy often directing their shot at them in particular."

"Our batteries were nothing more than old spars and timber laid up in parallel lines and filled between with mud and dirt.

"During the whole night, at intervals of a quarter or half an hour, the enemy would let off all their pieces, and although we had sentinels to watch them and at every flash of their guns to cry, 'a shot,' upon hearing which everyone endeavored to take care of himself, yet they would ever and anon, in spite of all our precautions, cut up some of us.

"The engineer in the fort was a French officer by the name of Fleury, the same who struck the British flag at the storming of Stony Point. [Fleury, it should be noted, was awarded a medal by Congress — a predecessor of the Medal of Honor — for that action.] He was a very austere man and kept us constantly employed day and night; there was no chance of escaping from his vigilance... We could watch an opportunity to escape from the vigilance of Colonel [sic] Fleury, and run into this place for a minute or two's respite from fatigue and cold. When the engineer found that the workmen began to grow scarce, he would come to the entrance and call us out. He had always his cane in his hand," Martin recalled, "and woe betided him he could get a stroke at.

"It was utterly impossible to lie down to get my rest or sleep on account of the mud, if the enemy shot would have suffered us to do so. Sometimes, some of the men, when overcome with fatigue and want of sleep, would slip away into the barracks to catch a nap of sleep, but it seldom happened that they all came out again alive.

"I will have just mention one thing which will show the apathy of our people at this time," he wrote. "We had, as I mentioned, before, a thirty-two pound cannon in the fort, but had not a single shot for it. The British also had one ... The artillery officers offered a gill of rum for each shot fired from that [British] piece, which the soldiers would procure. I have seen twenty to fifty men standing on the parade waiting with impatience the coming of the shot, which would often be seized before its motion had fully ceased and conveyed off to our gun to be sent back to its former owners.

"What little provisions we had was cooked by the invalids in our camp and brought to the island in old flour barrels; it was mostly corned beef and hard bread."

Friday, 14 November: "The soldiers," Martin recounted, "were all ordered to take their posts at the palisadoes, which they were ordered to defend to the last extremity ... The cannonade was severe ... Some of our officers endeavored to ascertain how many guns were fired in a minute by the enemy, but it was impossible, the fire was incessant."

In a letter to Varnum, after he took command, Thayer wrote: "By this I would give you to understand, that ye Cannonade we have here, we value not — nor can conceive how any one could dream of delivering up so important as this, at present from Cannons we have nothing to fear, if there should be no sudden Storms ...

"If Sir You will send us a reinforcement to Night, of 100 of more men twill certainly be a great means of ye salvation of this Garrison. A floating Battery of ye Enemy appear'd this morning — we have silenc'd her for ye present.

"P.S. A Boat with a Number of men deserted from our fleet but this Minute — they may give some favourable [account] of our state — insinuate some notions of evacuating ye Fort— —

"all well ... none hurt since my arrival here — the Garrison in good Spirits."

14-15 November: Replacements for the rest of the troops at Fort Mifflin arrive. These men include Varnum's "whole company of Artillery" [Captain Cook's Company]. Thayer reported the need for reinforcements or boats with which to get off the island.

The command of the Fort, until the end of the battle, was as follows: Major Simeon Thayer, 2nd Rhode Island; Major Fleury, engineer; Major Silas Talbot, 1st Rhode Island, "who commanded a reserve in the interior work" ... a kind of last retreat. The battery commanders are Captain James Lee, 2nd Continental Artillery, and Captain Edmund B. Dickinson. The only two men who served throughout the battle and who arrived with Smith were Major Fleury and Captain Lee.

Saturday, 15 November: Martin reported: "The whole area of the fort was as completely ploughed as a field. The buildings of every kind [were] hanging in broken fragments, and the guns all dismounted, and how many of the garrison sent to the world of spirits, I knew not. If ever destruction was complete, it was here."

At 6 p.m., Varnum wrote: "the fire is universal from the shipping and batteries. We have lost a great many men today; a great many officers are killed and wounded. My fine company of Artillery is almost destroyed. We shall be obliged to evacuate the fort this evening. Major Talbut [sic] is badly wounded. Major Fleury is wounded also."

Talbot remembered in later years that "the dead were rolled out of the way" of the guns.

Contrary to Varnum's on-the-spot reporting, Washington wrote to Alexander Hamilton that "the enemy have lately damaged Fort Mifflin considerably, but our people keep possession and seem to do so to the last extremity. Our loss in men has been but small, Capt. Treat is unfortunately among the killed."

At 7 p.m., Thayer dispatched all the garrison to Fort Mercer . . . except for 40 men. This small contingent spiked the cannon and destroyed everything the British might be able to use. They worked throughout the night.

Joseph Plumb Martin was one of the men left "to destroy and burn all that was left in the place. I was in the northwest battery," he wrote, "just after dark when the enemy were hauling their shipping on that side higher up to a more commanding position. They were so nigh that I could hear distinctly what they said on board the sloop.

"After the troop had left the fort and were embarking at the wharf, I went to the waterside to find one of my messmates to whom I had lent my canteen in the morning, as there were three or four hogsheads of rum in the fort, the heads of which were about to be knocked in, and I was desirous to save a trifle of their contents. There being nothing to eat I thought I might have something to drink."

Martin found his friend dead . . . "lying in a long row of dead men who had been brought out of the fort to be conveyed to the main, to have the last honors conferred upon them which it was in our power to give.

"I returned directly back into the fort to my party and proceeded to set fire immediately to the wharf where three batteaus were waiting to convey us across the river."

After the battle, 2 December, to be exact, General Henry Knox wrote Colonel John Lamb: "The defence of Fort Mifflin was as gallant as is to be found in history. Capt.-Lieutenant Treat, one of the most promising and best of young officers, was killed. Captain Lee has acquired great reputation in the defence of the fort. The last day of the siege, his company suffered much. His first lieutenant, two sergeants and three privates killed. One of the wounded men, a gunner, is Charles Proud."

Others who died included Captain Stephen Brown, 4th Connecticut, and Captain Nathan Stoddard, 8th Connecticut.

Sunday, 16 November: "A little after 2 a.m.," Thayer and the last men leave Fort Mifflin in "three batteaux." In one of the boats is Private Martin who provided one of the few accounts of Fort Mifflin's last hours: the fire, he wrote "threw such a light upon the water that we were as plainly seen by the British as though it had been broad day. Almost their whole fire was directed at us. Sometimes our boat seemed to be almost thrown out of the water, and a length of shot took the sternpost out of the rear boat. We had to stop and take the men from the crippled boat into the other two, and now the shot and water flew merrily, but by the assistance of a kind Providence we escaped" without any further injury and landed, a little after midnight, on the Jersey shore.

"We left our flag flying when we left the island, and the enemy did not take possession of the fort till late in the morning after we left. We left one man in the fort who had taken too large a dose of 'the good creature.' He was a deserter from the German forces in the British service," Martin recalled. "The British took him to Philadelphia, where not being known by them, he engaged again in their service, received two or three guineas bounty, drew a British uniform, and came back to us again at the Valley Forge."

Monday, 17 November: General Washington reported to the President of Congress: "I am sorry to inform you, that Fort Mifflin was evacuated the night before last, after a defence which does credit to the American Arms, and will ever reflect the highest honor upon the Officers and Men of the Garrison. The Works were entirely beat down, every piece of Cannon dismounted, and one of the Enemy's Ships so near, that she threw Grenades into the fort and killed the Men upon the platforms from her tops, before they quitted the Island . . .

"Nothing in the Course of this Campaign, has taken up so much of the attention and consideration of myself and all the General Officers, as the possibility of giving a further relief to Fort Mifflin, than what we had already afforded."

In retrospect, Joseph Plumb Martin wrote: "But there has been but little notice taken of it, the reason of which is, there was no Washington, Putnam, or Wayne there. Had there been, the affair would have been extolled to the skies . . . Great men get great praise; little men, nothing. But it always was so and always will be."

Thomas Paine in *Crisis V*: "The garrison, which scarce anything to cover them but their bravery, survived in the midst of mud, shot, and shells, and were at last obliged to give it up more to the powers of time and gunpowder than to military superiority of the besiegers."

Lord William Howe reported to the Right Honorable Lord George Germain from Philadelphia 28 November: "The Enemy's Fire upon the Ships of War, the Vigilant and Hulk from two floating Batteries, seventeen gallies and armed Vessels, and from a Battery on the Jersey Shore, was accordingly heavy, but the Gallantry displayed by the naval Commanders, their Officers and Seamen on this Occasion frustrated all their efforts, and contributed principally to the Reduction of the Enemy's Works . . .

"I have the Honor to enclose a return Nos. of the Cannon found in the Fort — the Enemy's Loss during the Siege is computed to have been 400 killed & wounded. The Loss to the Kings Troops was only seven killed and five wounded . . . ."

As I read the text of the pamphlet "A Fort Mifflin Diary," which I wrote in 1972 and which was published a year later by The Shackamaxon Society, of which I was president, I could not help but realize how much my writing was affected by the war in Vietnam. The more I read, the more I realized that the men of whom I wrote were no different . . . war was war.

I also realized that Washington's efforts were stymied many times during the war by petty jealousies and disagreements by his officers. Smith, who later commanded the defenses of Baltimore during the next war, emerges as a very petty man. D'Arendt, on the other hand, appears to be a coward. Could Fort Mifflin have held on longer? Could its defense have kept the British from supplying Philadelphia? After spending over ten years actively researching the fort and its history, I seriously doubt that its defenders could have held on any longer than they did. In fact, in retrospect, I am amazed that they held on as long as they did.

The personal accounts of the action at Fort Mifflin, particularly Joseph Plumb Martin's reflections, underscore a basic truth about America and the American military. To paraphrase General William C. Westmoreland . . . It's not the military that declares war, it's the politicians. And, it's the politicians, as we've seen here, who neglected to provide the Mifflin garrison with the materiel needed to do the politicians' biding.

Chapter Five————

Lydia Shunned the High Life

With the threat of British occupation of Philadelphia, patriotic propagandists publicized tales of the Hessians assaulting every woman in sight. The intent of these stories was to keep Philadelphians from fraternizing with the enemy and from giving them information on troop movements, food and more carnal creature comforts.

Notwithstanding the practiced exaggeration of some of the writers, the German mercenaries were attuned to the practice of "to the victor belong the spoils," and had practiced that dictum with great gusto in New Jersey the year before. Lord William Howe himself was not a prude by any stretch of the imagination. Howe and his contingent of officers took advantage of the vibrant young women who populated the colonial landscape. Howe's lady, — mistress would be a better word — Mrs. Elizabeth Loring, was a Boston import, not a Philadelphia product.

Despite his proclivity for the lady, Howe was first a soldier in command of enemy territory. In such a position, he had to require a certain amount of decorum on the part of his troops. Howe issued a decree that warned that any British soldier found guilty of raping an American woman would be hanged: any officer who got a local girl pregnant would be forced to marry her. Howe's rules, though strongly worded, were uneven in enforcement. Because of his amatory acts, Major William Shaw Cathcart, a close friend of Major Andre, was forced to marry Elizabeth Eliot, the daughter of a New York Tory. On the other hand, Captain Oliver DeLancey, a favorite with the Philadelphia lasses, sired two children without being forced to exchange nuptial vows with either mother.

Philadelphians didn't have to worry too much about rape — there were too many willing women in town. Despite the abundant supply, some British officers went so far as to advertise for girls, saying that a woman would "act in the capacity of housekeeper... Extravagant wages will be given, and no character required."

Though they worried about their women, the Quakers found solace in the abundance of British sterling which passed through their fingers. Rebecca Franks, a beauty in a day of lovely Philadelphia women, even tried to lure a close friend, the recent bride of William Paca, a signer of the Declaration of Independence from Maryland, to return to the city and play. "You have no idea of the continued amusement I live in," Rebecca wrote. "I scarce have a moment to myself. No loss for parties, even I am engaged to seven different gentlemen...."

With so many vivacious, available women, it is quite understandable why the British tarried so long in Philadelphia during the winter of 1777.

Later, the activities of these "enemy sympathizers" would be explained away as the actions of "young people in the bloom of life and spirit after being so long deprived of the gaieties and amusements of life which their ages and spirits called for...." The subject of politics, it was stressed, never was introduced into the conversations. It was merely a case of lusty women satisfying themselves in the arms of lusty men... men who just happened to wear the uniform of the enemy.

Not all the women took advantage of the situation and lived for the moment. Some remained faithful to the men who went off with General George Washington to fight for independence. One of these ladies, Lydia Darragh, quietly continued her support of the liberation movement long after Washington and his troops left Philadelphia. She had good reason: her 22-year-old son, Charles, was an officer, assigned to the commander-in-chief's staff.

During the occupation of Philadelphia, William Howe had his headquarters in the former residence of General John Cadwalader, "on the west side, the fourth door below Spruce Street" on Second Street. Cadwalader, as one will remember, was the general who delayed in crossing the Delaware and almost spoiled Washington's victory at Trenton. The British commandeered the Darragh house, across the street from Howe's headquarters, and ordered William Darragh, Lydia's husband, to find other accommodations for his family. Philadelphia that December was cold and crowded. Lydia was not going to take this order sitting down, so she strode across the street and demanded an audience with the general. While she waited, a member of Howe's staff began a conversation with her. As it turned out, they both were natives of Ireland. He asked Howe to amend the order. At first Howe declined because the British too were pressed for space. Finally, Howe decided to let the family stay, but to use one of the Darragh's rooms as a meeting place for councils of war. This arrangement didn't sit well with her. Not only was she to be inconvenienced, sending her younger children out of the city to the home of a relative of her husband, but also she had to have her house used as a meeting place for the planned destruction of freedom and her son.

Blessed with both an incurable curiosity and a mother's love for her son, Mrs. Darragh eavesdropped constantly on the British. Every tidbit of information she could overhear, she translated to cipher, sewed the encoded message into covered buttons, and sent it off to her son via members of the family.

On the night of 2 December, a British "officer came and told her to have all her family in bed at an early hour, as they wished to use the room that night free from interruption," as her daughter Ann recalled. "She promised to do so, and when all was quiet lay down herself, but could not sleep." Lydia Darragh experienced one of the unexplainable feelings of dread that mothers usually have about their offspring. While she worried, she heard loud voices coming from the council room. She got out of bed and went into a closet. As Ann Darragh described the closet, it was "separated from the council room by a thin board partition covered with paper . . . ." Lydia was just in time to hear British plans which frightened her. The enemy planned to surprise Washington at Whitemarsh "late in the evening of the 4th." Whitemarsh was where Charles was based, she realized. With a superior force and the element of surprise, the British victory was almost certain.

The attack, the way the British discussed it, was not to be a small one, but a massive move of more than 10,000 royal regulars. These troops, she learned, would be deployed along the Bethlehem Pike, above Chestnut Hill. From there, they would strike and snuff out the entire rebel army.

After hearing this, Mrs. Darragh went back to bed. When an officer knocked on her door to lock up the house, she didn't answer at first. According to Ann Darragh, "she did not answer until the third summons."

This information was so startling, Mrs. Darragh did not feel she could confide it to anyone else, nor could she endanger her family by letting them transport the warning. The next day she planned her action. Depending on which source one reads, Lydia told her husband she was going to use a pass to go to the country to see her children or go to a Frankford mill for flour. Her request did not arouse the suspicions of the officials — she had obtained passes from them for many such excursions.

With the contents of her overheard conversation reduced to memory, Lydia Darragh walked from her home on 2nd Street to Frankford and ordered her flour. She told the miller she would return for the sack later... after she paid a visit to her children.

Leaving Frankford, she went along the Nicetown Lane to within a mile of the Rising Sun Tavern, at the junction of the Germantown and York roads, where the Continental forces had an outpost. There she met Lieutenant-Colonel Thomas Craig of the Pennsylvania militia, an old family friend. Craig was surprised to see her. She asked him to escort her. He accompanied her for awhile, leading his horse. While they walked, she gave him her message. He then rushed off with the intelligence to Washington's headquarters. Before he left, Craig took her to a nearby house and "directed a female in it to give her something to eat." Lydia then returned to Philadelphia. She hadn't told her husband what she had done until she thought the danger had passed.

That night, Lydia Darragh sat and watched the unending redcoated lines of British troops march by her window. Even after they returned, she wasn't sure of what had happened. As a result of her "early warning," the British move was foiled and the troops returned to Philadelphia "like a parcel of damned fools." Her journey through the snow and wind, along rough country roads, had paid off. Washington, though he never knew the source of the intelligence, owed his life to Lydia Darragh.

The next night, a British officer came to the Darragh house and ordered Lydia Darragh into the council room. He locked the door. Were the members of your family awake on the night of the British council? he asked. "No," she responded, "they were all in bed and asleep." Then he said: "I need not ask you, for we had great difficulty in waking you to fasten the door after us. But one thing is certain;

the enemy had notice of our coming, were prepared for us, and we marched back like a parcel of damned fools. The walls," he decided ironically, "must have ears." In later days, Lydia Darragh would smile when she recalled that night. "I never told a lie about it," she would say. "I could answer all his questions without that."

The tale of this fine Quaker lady was first published by Robert Walsh in an 1827 issue of the *American Quarterly Review*. Walsh's account was based on information given him by friends of the Darragh family. John Fanning Watson, author of *Watson's Annals of Philadelphia*, continued the story, based on material he had received from Hannah Marshall Haines of Germantown. Lydia's daughter, Ann, related the story to her family. At the time of the incident, Ann would have been 21. Elias Boudinot recalled the event in his *Memoirs* in every detail . . . but one: he neglected to mention the lady by name. The Lydia Darragh story had once been taught in the Philadelphia public school system. It has since been relegated to the status of a romantic tale.

It is ironic that Lydia Darragh's story has been forgotten since the accuracy of her acts is based on the same type of evidence — a hand-me-down story — that prompted the legend of Betsy Ross. At the same time, we can think of Lydia Darragh's historic slight as a standoff. After all, the children in Philadelphia's public schools don't learn about the frolicking activities of their Loyalist-leaning ancestors, either.

There was a time when Philadelphia's school children learned about Lydia Darragh, and how she helped save George Washington. There is, in fact, a school named in her honor. But, some rigid bureaucrat took the tale and dismissed it — forever — because there weren't too many written accounts of her escapades. The basis for the Darragh story had as much credibility as did the Betsy Ross flag story. Each was based on tradition, rather than definitive fact. Jim Smart, who was one of the brightest columnists for The Evening Bulletin, used to rebel at the academic approach to things. Why is it, he would ask, do they require you to put down documentary evidence when the proof is what my grandmother told me? History, as far as Jimmy was concerned, had to begin somewhere. Someone had to say something that someone else wrote down. You know something? He was absolutely right.

It really was a shame that they excised Lydia because there are too few female heroes [or heroines] in the pages of our Revolutionary War history books. To remind people in 1977 about Lydia was my way of helping to right a wrong.

Darley's drawing of the American Army marching to Valley Forge, 20 miles northwest of Philadelphia. Accounts of the starvation and suffering at Valley Forge may have been inflated, as subsequent archeological research shows that the officers ate well during the encampment.

Chapter Six————

Tactical Ideal/Human Disaster

By 19 December 1777, the American army was "not only starved but naked," Private Joseph Plumb Martin remembered. "The greatest were not only shirtless and barefoot, but destitute of all other clothing, especially blankets."

It was in this condition that the men from the defeats at Brandywine and Germantown, and the valiant defense of the Delaware River forts arrived at Valley Forge.

From a tactical point of view, Valley Forge was an ideal location for a winter encampment. It had an abundant water supply, was in an excellent defensive position — midway between the British in Philadelphia and the Continental Congress at York, Pennsylvania, and it was surrounded by dense, heavily wooded areas which could provide firewood and building materials. But, from the human standpoint, Valley Forge was a disaster. There were no villages or farms nearby, to provide food, and no shelter whatsoever . . . except for the stone mansions which Washington and his senior staff immediately appropriated for themselves. [It was interesting when, during the preparations for the Bicentennial, that state archeologists uncovered countless chicken carcasses in and around the dig at Varnum's headquarters. The discovery modified much of the thinking about the starvation suffered at Valley Forge.]

"To see men without clothes to cover their nakedness," Washington wrote, "without blankets to lie on, without shoes by which their marches might be traced by the blood from their feet, and almost so often without provisions as with them, marching through the frost and snow, and at Christmas taking up their winter quarters within a day's march of the enemy without a house or hut over them, till they could be built, and submitting to it without a murmur, is proof of patience and obedience which in my opinion can scarce be paralleled."

It was more than patience and obedience which sustained the Continental Army. It was a matter of individual and national survival. If Washington's men wanted to live through the winter of 1777-78, they would fell trees and build the cabins. They would forage throughout the countryside to supplement their meager rations. Most of them did. Many could not. Out of the ten thousand men who were bivouacked at Valley Forge, twenty-five hundred died of disease, malnutrition and exposure to the elements.

While the American soldiers suffered and died at their winter camp, Pennsylvania farmers were getting rich selling their produce to the British in Philadelphia. English sterling was more important to them than Continental script — or American lives.

"Private contractors reaped a golden harvest," one contemporary wrote, "by sending hundreds of government wagons north from Pennsylvania loaded with flour and iron while pork in Jersey awaiting shipment to the army spoiled for lack of transport." The food rotted and the merchants grew fat, but the soldiers made do with what they had.

One officer at Valley Forge noticed a soldier cooking some unknown substance over an open fire. What do you have in your pot, he asked the man?

"A stone," the soldier answered, "for they say there is some strength in stone, if you can only get it out."

The suffering of these fighting men was uncalled for. It was, as many contended, the result of American mismanagement, graft, speculation, and indifference. Congress, some charged, could provide rag to make money — but not for a stitch of clothing for the soldiers.

Despite the privations, the private soldier endured. "We have engaged in the defence of our injured country," Private Martin concluded, "and were willing, nay, we were determined to persevere as long as such hardships were not altogether intolerable."

One can only wonder how an ill-fed, ill-clad disorganized mob of citizen soldiers — with little visible support from their fellow-citizens — could ultimately defeat the superior British forces. Perhaps the belief in the concepts of Liberty and Independence, shared by the common soldier, sustained them more than food and clothing.

Valley Forge always fascinated me. My first full-scale memory of it was when I attended the Boy Scout Jamboree there in the Fifties. Even then I couldn't figure out why Valley Forge held such an important place in American history. There was no battle fought there. In more modern terms, it was rear echelon all the way. The tales I had heard about the bloodstained tracks in the snow produced disgust in me and further indicated that leadership was deplorable . . . but I was, and am, in a minority regarding the way some of our history is perceived and presented by historians. In this piece, which appeared as part of a series I wrote for The Evening Bulletin I tried to balance the myths with reality. I tried to show that while the common soldier was starving, someone was eating chicken at General James M. Varnum's headquarters and, as you will read later, George and Martha Washington had trouble getting table linen for their dinner table, even though their waiter was half-naked. Though to some people such discoveries should be left hidden, I feel they are part of the fabric of our lives. We should know about these things. We should realize our leaders are not gods, that they are human just like the rest of us. And, if our leaders would only come to the same realization . . . .

General George Washington. This illustration, first published in Harper's Weekly, 4 May 1889, was adapted from a Charles Willson Peale painting. Peale produced a series of paintings of Washington — from a single sitting with different backgrounds.

Chapter Seven————

Washington on Bended Knee

Tradition has it that in the early weeks at Valley Forge, a frustrated, demoralized George Washington was discovered kneeling, alone in the snow, with his head bowed deep in prayer. The pose, the worshipping general, was commemorated on the 1977 Christmas stamp. Is it a true portrait of the man who led a band of undisciplined men through hell and high water to independence? Or is it, like the "I cannot tell a lie" story of Parson Mason L. Weems, an after-creation of legend-making people?

No one has ever located documentary evidence, such as eyewitness accounts of the pose depicted on the stamp. But even with the lack of substantiation it does not mean that the event did not take place. Based on what is known about the religious spirit of George Washington, it is probable that he did engage in private reflection — whether it be called prayer or some other descriptive phrase.

A baptized member of the Church of England — the acceptable church of the times, Washington attended worship services of that denomination during his youth and young manhood. He served as vestryman and warden of his home church. He was not, however, a confirmed member of the Church of England. But that was through no fault of his own. The circumstances of the times precluded it.

There were no bishops in colonial America [The first Episcopal prelate in this country was Bishop William White of Philadelphia, and he didn't become a bishop until after the war.] and any Episcopalian who wanted to receive the "laying on of hands" had to journey to England. Few — only the most affluent — took the trouble. Baptism and faith were adequate for the majority of American members of the Anglican Church.

When Washington married, it was according to the rites of his church. And, throughout his life, he remained a member of the church of his youth. But Washington was also a creature of his times. The Enlightenment had created doubt in men's minds. The thinkers of his day refrained from calling the Being Outside Themselves "God." They were more comfortable with other titles, like "Providence." Washington was comfortable with Providence and used the word frequently in his writings. His beliefs were also a blend of Roman Stoicism, the closest classic philosophy to Christianity, and Christianity itself. Senaca, the chief spokesman for the Stoics, used the word "Providence" frequently in his writings.

Though most religious leaders would object to his lack of orthodoxy, Washington himself wanted everyone to be free to practice religion as that individual saw fit. "Being no bigot myself to any mode of worship," he wrote to the Marquis de Lafayette, "I am disposed to indulge the professors of Christianity in the church, that road to heaven which to them shall seem the most direct, plainest, easiest, and least liable to exception." He did not care to what sect a person belonged. He was more concerned that an individual should adhere to some code of personal moral conduct.

At Valley Forge, he put his words into action. He ordered morning prayers and Sunday morning services and urged enlisted men and officers alike to attend with some regularity. He endeavored to instill in the men under his command the value of Christian character. He made public prayer routine and, to make it more important to his men, followed it with the reading of daily orders and roll call.

Faith was an important ingredient to his concept of the Continental Army. It was so important that he stated in one of his orders issued at the encampment: "To the distinguished character of a Patriot, it should be our highest glory to add the more distinguished character of a Christian." To further his ends, he encouraged Congress to import 20,000 Bibles to be distributed to the troops. Since there was little to read that winter, it can be assumed that the men made use of them. And, the chaplains that Washington corralled to preach to his men, provided another diversion to their monotonous existence.

Was George Washington sincere? Was he really seen with his head bowed in prayer on that windswept hill at Valley Forge? Does it really matter? What is important is that the man portrayed provided a rag-tag, bob-tail band of men with a shining example of faith. He did everything within his power to demonstrate that faith can conquer many obstacles. [Years later, I met Captain Eugene "Red" McDaniel, USN [Ret.], a former prisoner of war from the Vietnam War. Red proved, during his six years in captivity, that a military person can never lose faith in his God, his country, or himself.] Washington's example rubbed off.

The Continental soldiers went to worship services and they prayed and — most important — they believed. They believed in God, Providence, or whatever name they gave to the Being Outside Themselves. And that belief caused them to have faith in the justice of their cause and the men leading them. Their faith was not misplaced — it resulted, finally, in the British surrender at Yorktown.

If you have one around, look at the 1977 Christmas stamp. See in it what you want. See in it a man praying according to the standard rote of a traditional sect. Or see in it a man who created his own words of communication. Whichever the case, you will see a man who believed in Providence and placed himself under that guidance and power . . . And Providence blessed him.

I am very proud of the Freedoms Foundation Gold Medal that I received a number of years back. In fact, I usually wear a replica of the medal in my buttonhole. Like many other Americans, I believed that the depiction of George Washington on my medal was that of a man bent over in prayer. Even though I thought I believed it, I was not quite sure. After all, the men of the Revolution were not traditional believers, they were men who had been "enlightened." It was possible that they didn't practice "religion" as we do today. Not until I dug into the historical data did I come up with a more realistic story. As one can imagine, this was not a popular article . . . especially when it was first published 27 December 1977 in The Evening Bulletin.

Chapter Eight

A Man's Place is in the Home

The Continental Army, that stalwart band of brave patriots, was not always what the history books lead us to believe.

"Our army," George Washington once conceded to a friend, "is shamefully reduced by desertion, and except that the people in the country can be forced to give information when deserters return to their old neighborhoods, we shall be obliged to detach one half the army to bring the other back." In Philadelphia, the *Pennsylvania Ledger* reported that deserters were coming into Philadelphia so rapidly that Howe would soon be able to fight Washington with his own army.

The commander-in-chief could never be certain from day to day exactly how many men he could muster. When the harvest was due, men left. After all, they were citizens first, soldiers second. Many Continental soldiers, though resourceful and daring in battle, were neither disciplined nor dependable between engagements.

The officers to whom they reported and who ordered them into battle were friends and hometown neighbors. The private soldier selected his company officers and, by so doing, selected men who were friends — or someone who thought the same way he did. A good friend, the soldier thought, was one who understood that a man's place was in the home — at least during planting and reaping.

Unfortunately, wars and battles were not won with irresponsible, absent troops. The mass exodus of men had to cease. To cope with this serious problem, and staunch the flow, Washington and his cadre of officers began to punish any wrongdoer who was captured. The object of the punishment — which was conducted publicly — was to set an example for all the other soldiers. By watching a comrade-in-arms being humiliated, Washington thought, the common soldier would think twice before attempting the same thing himself. There were no psychological punishments, other than being made to stand and watch; all were corporal. The ultimate penalty sometimes seemed more humane than the public whippings.

For desertion, the prescribed punishment was 78 lashes; for thievery, 39. The basis for the quantity of strokes was determined by the officers from reading the Bible, especially St. Paul's letter to the Corinthians, in which Paul wrote: "Of the Jews five times received I 40 stripes save one." It is interesting to note that many of the punishments for crimes during the early days of this country were determined from biblical dictate. Reading the Bible was one of the few luxuries of camp life during the Revolution. But public admonishments did not stem the flow of deserters. The men who left the camps thought they were smarter than the ones who had been punished; they wouldn't get caught.

As the officers became more and more frustrated by the rate of desertion and the mutinies, they looked for more cruel and bizarre punishments that would set the best possible example. When three deserters from the 1st Pennsylvania Regiment were captured, the soldiers wanted to kill them on the sport. That would really do no good, calmer minds thought. After some discussion, it was decided to let the prisoners draw lots; the loser would have his head cut off. After the beheading, the deserter's head was placed on a pole and carried by the other two into camp and its final resting place — over the gallows. It stood as a warning to everyone in camp.

In another case, as recounted by Ebenezer Wild in his journal, a group of condemned soldiers were marched to the place of execution with their coffins before them. After the death sentence had been read, and the graves dug, the men were made to kneel before their final resting places.

The executioners, men drawn from the condemned's former units, were ordered to "Load. Take Aim . . . ." At that crucial point, a messenger ran up and announced that a reprieve had been granted. This was neither the first nor the last time a reprieve was issued at the eleventh hour. But no one could ever be certain.

That was the lesson: a soldier could never take the chance of being dead wrong.

In some circles, it is almost considered unpatriotic to speak about what went on at Valley Forge, besides the starvation and agony of the Continental Army. But other things were happening, things that usually go untold. The desertions were one of the things that have been ignored. I can't think of one study that's been conducted that deals with the subject. In later years, I've done a great deal of research on military discipline, specifically the courts-martial procedures of the Civil War. I've learned that it doesn't matter which war it is, the dispensation of military justice is swift and, sometimes, it isn't justice at all.

A miniature portrait of Martha Washington. She put her personal fears aside to provide comfort to her husband during the winter of 1777-78.

Chapter Nine——————

Softening a Harsh Winter

After George Washington's men had built huts at Valley Forge to his satisfaction, the general moved into more spacious quarters — the farmhouse of Deborah Hewes. It was to this small home that Martha Washington came to be with her husband in early February 1778.

Martha really didn't want to make the trip from Virginia to Pennsylvania. Travel, strange places and guns frightened her — frightened her more than she ever let on to her husband. But the wedding vows "to love, honor and obey" her spouse were stronger than the innate fears that plagued her and drew her lips into a fine line.

Besides her fears, fate had not been kind to Mrs. Washington. she had lost her father, husband, three of her four children and, most recently, her beloved sister, Fanny Bassett. Fanny, the general's wife wrote to Burwell Bassett, had been "the greatest favorite I had in the world. If to meet our departed friends and know them was certain, we could have very little reason to desire to stay in this world," she added, "for I wish for more sincerely than to be with you . . . ." But she could not. Washington had told her he would send for her and her primary duty was to her husband. "If he does," she wrote, "I must go."

Typically male, Washington did not think of the devils that pressured his wife. Rather he thought of the creature comforts she would expect. Washington feared Martha would find his headquarters "a dreary kind of place, and uncomfortably provided." To improve things, he tried to locate his baggage, which had been abandoned before the fall of Philadelphia. He salvaged enough for Martha to begin housekeeping.

Martha Washington came to the Forge and found Deborah Hewes' farmhouse quite tiny. The structure was so small that the rooms in which the general's aides slept at night had to be evacuated in the morning to serve as sitting rooms for visitors. Martha did not complain but began to work at converting the all-male enclave into some semblance of a home.

In an attempt to make life more tolerable for his wife, Washington built a log cabin adjacent to the main house where the staff and family could dine. But a private dining room did not guarantee elegant dining in the Virginia tradition to which Martha was so accustomed. Washington tried, but with little success. "I cannot get as much cloth," he complained, "as will make clothes for my servants." One of the men, the general noted, "attends my person and table . . . indecently and most shamefully naked." It should be noted that Washington also noted that his men were walking about naked and leaving trails of blood from their unshod feet.

Notwithstanding the lack of proper appointments to his table and the pressure of command, George Washington was a different man than when he first arrived at Valley Forge. The reason was Martha. Her presence soothed and calmed her husband and provided him with inner strength. Washington had always had enemies but, because of Martha's pleasant demeanor, difficulties were smoothed over quickly.

Martha Washington was a woman of dignity; yet, at the same time, she was totally unassuming. She never gossiped or came up with the witty comments ladies at court were want to produce. Her charm and simple approach put others at ease. Martha was unpretentious. Women thought of her as one of them — as an equal, never a threat. She did not talk about the battles, the strategies, but focused on childrearing and domestic chores — things that she knew best. Perhaps it was because of her fears or lack of knowledge that she didn't expound on other things. Whichever the case, conversation with her was a pleasant respite. People could talk with her and know that she would keep a confidence. In a command post, this was a rarity. Once someone talked things over with her, the problems never seemed to be so bad as they were originally.

The men with whom she came in contact were also taken with her — from enemy to ally. A Hessian prisoner thought she was "pretty"; while Chastellux, the French general, commented she looked "like a German princess." Another Frenchman remarked "her appearance is respectable; she was dressed plainly and her manners were simple in all respects." Martha Washington "reminded me of the Roman matrons of whom I had read so much," Pierre Du Ponceau wrote, "and I thought that she well deserved to be the companion and friend of the greatest man of the age."

Because she came to Valley Forge, other military wives rushed to their husbands' sides at Washington's headquarters. The introduction of ladies to the otherwise boring surroundings brightened the commander's life and made his cares seem less onerous. It seems unlikely that the other wives would have come to the army camp if the general's wife had not gone there first. Military protocol did not allow for individual action. Each subordinate follows the lead of his superior in more than battle. He tries to emulate his leader in manner, apparel, and if a wife should be at his side or not. Washington, it is sure, realized this when he summoned Martha. Officers who have their wives at their side are less likely to request leave — or seek dalliances elsewhere. One must wonder, however, what effect the presence of these women had on the enlisted soldier, the man who could not bring his wife to camp.

Washington also realized what a prize he had in Martha. He knew her quiet ways would eliminate many of the problems of day-to-day army life, and that the morale of his officer corps would improve. But, most important of all, Washington knew that his life was empty without Martha. She brought to him the inner calm he needed. She brought warmth to his cold headquarters and love to his weary heart. Martha's qualities helped him endure the remainder of the winter, the battles to come . . . and the joy of ultimate victory.

Tradition tells us that, for most of the men at Valley Forge, the winter was horrendous. The privations were intensified by the absence of their loved ones. But, not all the soldiers were deprived. As we noted earlier, archeologists located chicken bones in their dig at Varnum's headquarters. Rank had its privilege . . . in more ways than one. Senior officers, for the most part, were able to invite their wives — or women — to visit. George Washington was no exception. In fact, Washington set the stage by bringing Martha to the camp. In his own mind, he saw nothing wrong in her prolonged visit. It was important to Washington that his wife ease his life. But, did the appearance of Martha Washington at Valley Forge ease the common soldiers' mind? This is a question I cannot answer. In reviewing the research, I could not find one negative comment about Martha's visit.

Baron Frederick William Augustus von Steuben, a former Prussian soldier, who, veterans of the Revolution wrote, was "capable of forming the whole world into a solid column, and deploying it from the center." Illustration from Chappel's painting of von Steuben on horseback.

Chapter Ten————

Molding an Army

The scent of battle on the American continent, mingled with an opportunity for riches and personal glory, enticed many European
military men to come to the aid of the Continental Army.

In another time and another place, our collective conscience
would have recoiled at the thought that foreigners would be allowed
to involve themselves in a war outside their own shores — and in-
terests. But, during the Revolution, America needed the expertise and
knowledge of "technical advisers" — "soldiers of fortune," if you
will — from abroad. And it was forthcoming.

Pierre Beaumarchais, better known as the author of "The Barber
of Seville," operated a small company that was organized as a con-
duit for the shipment of French arms and munitions to the besieged
colonists. With the concurrence and connivance of highly-placed
government officials, Beaumarchais also recruited these "soldiers of
fortune" to help train the raw American recruits and look after their
equipment. These advisers, actually professional soldiers, were
ultimately followed by French might — troops, equipment and munitions. [This practice is one which in modern days has come under great
fire, particularly in the case of the Nicaraguan "contras."]

One "adviser," so recruited, was Baron Frederick William

Augustus von Steuben. It is possible — more likely probable — that the Prussian soldier entered the service of this country under false credentials. The "von" of his name was inserted by his social-climbing father, and the "baron" title he bore was an adopted, not awarded, honor. But, unlike some of the other foreign volunteers, von Steuben had some military experience — not so much, though, as Silas Deane and Benjamin Franklin intimated to George Washington and the Congress when they recommended him. In reality, at the time of the American Revolution, von Steuben was an aging man, deeply in debt and forgotten by most, if not all, his friends.

In his own words, he was "extremely anxious to have an encounter either in Hades, or at the head of a regiment." It didn't matter which king or which congress he served. His own personal glory and professional pride were of greater importance to him than mere patriotic sentiments. He was born a soldier and black powder surged through his bloodstream. Upon his arrival in America, Frederick von Steuben was much like the ancient quarterback who runs out on the field looking to score that one last great touchdown, achieve that one last triumph which will assure him of a place in the Hall of Fame.

Yet the reasons behind von Steuben's determination to serve in America didn't matter when he finally arrived at Valley Forge 23 February 1778. Faced with a rag-tag, bob-tail mob of men, von Steuben drilled them until they were soldiers who "knew perfectly how to bear arms, had a military air, knew how to march, to form in columns, deploy, and execute some little maneuvers with excellent precision."

It is a human trait to recall events from the past in the most favorable light. Men can recall the good times, never the bad. That was not the case with the Prussian officer. In his memoirs, he remembered the nights of despair as well as the days of joy. Despite doubts about his former training and experience and his use of unearned titles, von Steuben took the unskilled citizen-soldiers and turned them into a dynamic, disciplined army.

Was it necessary for von Steuben to actually be a baron? Was it necessary that he be a member of royalty? Or was it more important that he be an able instructor? The proof of what he accomplished is best contained in the "Creed Adopted by Officers of the American Army" in 1792:

"We believe that George Washington is the only fit man to head the American Army," the veterans wrote, "that Baron Steuben has made us soldiers, and that he is capable of forming the whole world into a solid column, and deploying it from the center. We believe in his Blue Book . . . and we believe in our bayonets. Amen."

Without von Steuben and others like him — the Marquis de Lafayette, Thaddeus Kosciuszko, Casmir Pulaski, Cosmo de Medici — "technical advisers" — this nation might not have achieved its freedom.

When this article first appeared 28 February 1978, The Evening Bulletin received a few letters from readers who were upset that I stated that "von" Steuben's credentials were less than authentic when he signed up to work for Washington. What they didn't realize was that people sometimes think they can accomplish more if someone thinks they're something they're not. This is not solid reasoning. Von Steuben proved that a commoner could train raw troops just as well as a royalist.

In retrospect, I wondered why people didn't complain about the "advisers" who helped in the American cause. Was it not wrong for the French government to help stage a war against Great Britain? Was is all right for other countries to help the colonies, but not the other way around?

Chapter Eleven———

A "Paddy" at Valley Forge

The winter was just over. The American soldiers could feel a new strength filling their bodies. They were happy; they had survived disease, deprivations and the cold of Valley Forge. At the same time, they were bored. During the winter, their attention was constantly focused on survival. There was now little to keep them busy, except for the constant drilling under Baron von Steuben. Being soldiers, they looked for a little excitement . . . anything at all.

They amused themselves as best they could with crafts and games. They played checkers, carved from wood or made from smashed musket balls. The more adventuresome troopers wagered cards if they had them, or dice fabricated from bullets. And they conceived pranks that only bored soldiers can dream up.

As St. Patrick's Day, a very important day for the Irish soldiers, approached, the German-Americans found the ideal vehicle for some mischief to end all mischief. The Germans of the Pennsylvania battalion created a "Paddy." A "Paddy" was a stuffed representation of St. Patrick. A dummy was made and dressed in scraps of green and white material to symbolize the Irish colors. Topping off the dummy, complete with a bulbous nose, were the trappings of a bishop — a cope, mitre and crook. The Germans thought they had done an excellent job.

On the night of 16 March, the Germans stole into the Irish camp-site and deposited their work of art. When the Irish awoke and viewed the grotesque "Paddy," they saw red. An Irishman can laugh at his own foibles, but never at jibes directed toward his patron saint. No Catholic, they decided, would be so sacrilegious to create such an affront. It could only be the work of a Protestant, and not just any Protestant, but one of those who didn't believe in the authority of bishops. Therefore, they reasoned, it had to be the sinful work of the ultra-Protestants — the Presbyterians from New England.

With fire in their eyes and might in their hands, the Irish approached as a body against the unsuspecting New Englanders . . . much to the amusement of their compatriots in Catholicism, the Germans. The entire Continental Army was going to witness a battle . . . one bigger than the ones they fought at Brandywine or Germantown. Trouble was imminent as the fighting-mad Irish faced off at the mystified New England Protestants.

Through his subordinates, Washington had learned of the machinations of the Germans. At the critical moment of confrontation, the general rode in among them, before the first drop of blood was shed. Washington knew the identity of the culprits, but he also knew it wasn't the right time to make a full disclosure. With all the tact that his military experience could muster, the commander-in-chief turned the entire episode into a joke. He told the assembled men that he was an ardent admirer of St. Patrick and would like to celebrate the day in a proper manner. And he wanted all to participate. To establish the holiday spirit, he had an extra ration of whiskey issued to every soldier.

The Irish felt that it would be a more fitting celebration if they toasted the good saint than if they fought over him. So Valley Forge relaxed and Irish and German and English and every possible combination of ancestry drank themselves into friendship.

In Philadelphia, the Irish troops, members of His Majesty's Own who guarded the Broad Street Prison, were also in a festive St. Patrick's Day mood. They drank and sang, just like the Irish at Valley Forge. But His Majesty's Own were so intent on commemorating St. Patrick's deeds that they failed to notice a small group of American prisoners who "borrowed" the cell keys . . . and escaped.

It didn't matter on which side an Irishman fought. On St. Patrick's Day, he was Irish first . . . a Britisher or Continental second.

I always thought St. Patrick's Day was invented by the New York Irish as an excuse to parade up and down Fifth Avenue — and get drunk — not necessarily in that order. Was I surprised back in 1978, when I researched this article. I found that the celebration of St. Patrick's Day went back in time — long before the American Revolution. And, it was a very important day for the Irish even then. As I read and wrote, I could see why the Irish were so upset and how Washington reasoned upon the best solution.

Chapter Twelve─────

Washington's Spy Network

As commander-in-chief of the Continental Army, George Washington was aware of the need for quick, reliable information — intelligence — and encouraged the use of "secret agents" to obtain it.

The first American "central intelligence agency" probably began on 30 December 1776, when Washington requested Robert Morris to send "hard money — to pay a certain Set of People who are of particular use to us." Morris quickly dispatched what he had on hand: "410 Spanish dollars, two English crowns, 10 shillings six-pence, and a French half crown." The information gathering system was officially in operation.

The first intelligence "director" was Nathaniel Sackett. Washington told him on 4 February 1777 to get "the earliest and best Intelligence of the designs of the Enemy." In return, Sackett would receive $50 a month and an additional $500 to pay for the services and expenses of his agents. Two months later, General Thomas Mifflin set up a spying system in Philadelphia. It was well-planned and, by the time Sir William Howe took over the city, the net was functioning and relaying information to Washington.

The commander-in-chief was selective in his choice of intelligence agents. He didn't want amateurs... "Give the persons you pitch upon," he instructed Mifflin, "proper lessons . . . " and choose "some in the Quaker line, who have never taken an active part, (these) would be least liable to suspicion."

Due to pressures and problems, Mifflin turned over the reins of his operation to Major John Clark, Colonel Elias Boudinot, Captain Charles Craig, and Major Allan McLane. Their operatives continued to relay confidential material to Washington . . . under the cloak of great secrecy. As a result, most members of the Philadelphia spy community were never identified. There were, however, a few exceptions.

Lydia Darragh was one. And there was "Mom" Rinker, a young woman who bleached her flax atop a high rock above the Wissahickon Valley in what is now Philadelphia's Fairmount Park. She would sit on her rock for hours, knitting. There was nothing suspicious about her actions. Everyone . . . British and colonials alike . . . could see her. "Mom" would secret her information within the ball of knitting yarn; and, at the right moment, let the ball drop — over the edge of the cliff. Later, when the coast was clear, American couriers would deliver the contents to Washington.

Another pair of local undercover agents were Jacob and John Levering, who scouted the countryside between Manyunk and Philadelphia, along the Wissahickon. Posing as a Quaker farmer, Jacob made frequent trips through the British lines. He openly canoed down the Schuylkill to Philadelphia, where he acquired needed intelligence by selling produce door-to-door.

Spying was — and is — a dangerous occupation. Colonel Elias Dayton had two outstanding agents working between New York and New Jersey — the Hendricks brothers, John and Baker. In late January 1778, both men, along with John Meeker, were arrested by the colonials for "illegal Correspondence with the Enemy." The three agents, protecting the secrecy of their operation, stood silent — while their countrymen prepared to execute them.

In an attempt to protect his sources — and their lives, Dayton appealed directly to Washington. The general, in turn, wrote in confidence to New Jersey's governor, William Livingston, noting that the three spies would have to "bear the suspicion of being thought inimical, and it is not in their powers to assert their innocence, because that would get abroad and destroy the confidence which the Enemy puts in them." Would the governor do something?

No record exists as to what Livingston actually did, but the three agents were back in operation by February 1778 . . . and they were still conveying information three years later — with no one the wiser.

With well-oiled precision, the American spy network continued to relay its information to headquarters.

On 13 May 1778, Washington knew that Clinton was scheduled to replace Sir William Howe, even though Howe had only resigned two days earlier. Now General Washington wanted to know what the British were going to do. He was certain they planned to evacuate Philadelphia . . . but where were they going from here? Would they give up the colonies completely? Would they go to New York . . . by sea . . . or overland through New Jersey?

By the end of May, Washington's intelligence pointed to an exodus to New York. A spy in Chester reported a fleet of one hundred sails leaving Philadelphia. Allen McLane's cavalry rode close to the city and confirmed the port was empty.

George Washington had a smooth intelligence operation. His sources filtered in information with great regularity. Because of the secrecy, many of these men and women remained anonymous . . . forgotten heroes of the War for Independence.

While I was researching this particular piece, the American intelligence community was going through another microscopic inspection. At the time, I was using as a reference a book by New York lawyer William Casey. Little was I to know that a few years later he would run Ronald Reagan's presidential campaign, become the director of the Central Intelligence Agency, and, before his death, be embroiled as a key figure in the Iran-Contra mess.

My research has shown me, nonetheless, that spying is as old as mankind. Anyone who's ever read the Bible will recall evidence of covert action in both the Old and the New Testaments. Washington was just following an ancient tradition.

Chapter Thirteen————

The Shad Starts Running

The winter snows of 1777-78 were rapidly becoming memories. No longer were the rough footpaths of Valley Forge hidden beneath the cloying white blankets. Spring was calming the chilling winds, warming the frozen earth.

Washington's men could feel the squish of mud beneath their feet. Wild garlic, chicory and dandelion poked their shoots upward, only to be uprooted and reappear in cooking pots throughout the camp. The men of George Washington's ragged army began to think life was not over for them — there was hope and there was a future.

General Nathanael Greene was named quartermaster general in early March and proceeded to put the men to work. Under his direction, the troops scoured the countryside for wagons that had been abandoned along the roads months before on the journey to Valley Forge. They cannibalized those that were beyond repair and transformed the remainder into a fleet of serviceable vehicles. Engineers were dispatched to repair the roads and bridges between the Forge and Lancaster. Tools and equipment were scrounged from barns and farmhouses around the perimeter of the camp.

By mid-April, through the assistance of Jeremiah Wadsworth, commissary general, food arrived. For the first time in many months, the common soldier could pat his belly and know it was there. The daily allowance now was a pound-and-a-half of bread, a pound of fish, beef or pork and beans, and . . . a gill of whiskey. Clothing, weapons and ammunition followed shortly.

To speed the flow of supplies, General John Sullivan and his New Hampshire men built a bridge across the Schuylkill River near Fatlands Ford, a short distance from the mouth of Valley Creek. Sullivan's Bridge was not the wonder of the century, but 12 feet wide and of rough construction, it was adequate to accommodate men and wagons.

As the sun warmed the earth and river, the American shad began their annual pilgrimage upriver to spawn. Prized for their roe, the shad had made the hazardous journey through the British lines to the delight of the American troops. The waters of the Schuylkill boiled and churned as hundreds of soldiers beat the surface with sticks and tree limbs, shepherding the fish into nets. Realizing the shad might be a source of food for the Americans, the British had briefly considered destroying the river ladders used by the shad to ascend the Schuylkill's falls. But the British decided the fish weren't that strong. They felt the same way about the American soldiers.

The once-starving Continental Army stuffed itself with the patriotic fish. And those that were not eaten were barreled in salt and preserved for a future day.

To remind the men of hardships ahead, Congress, in its infinite wisdom, declared 22 April 1778 as a "day of Fasting, humiliation, and Prayer." Fasting, humiliation and prayer were not new ideas to the men at Valley Forge. They didn't really need a special day of commemoration. But they didn't complain. It was a holiday and no work was expected of them that day.

Under Washington and the volatile von Steuben, the troops had attained some measure of discipline. But they were still citizen-soldiers, not puppets of some foreign power. Officers, instead of setting an example for their men, demanded the perquisites and privileges of their rank, one of which was a mount. Washington's officers were supposed to supply their own horses. Besides being a necessary means of movement, horses were a mark of prestige. Officers continued amassing them until the herd at Valley Forge exhausted the forage supply. Over 1,500 horses starved to death in the camp. The weak soldiers were unable to help them, or even to bury the carcasses. And the fetid flesh of once-strong steeds rotted on the ground.

As the weather continued to improve, dissension mounted.

Regularly-commissioned officers disliked the militia commanders, feeling they outranked them. Together, the troops resented all the foreigners — except for young Lafayette. Soldiers from different states and different parts of the same states distrusted each other. Colonel Persifor Frazier of Pennsylvania thought New Englanders to be "low, dirty, cowardly, lying rascals." On the other hand, Joseph Plumb Martin of Connecticut would rather have been "incorporated with a tribe of western Indians as with any of the southern troops." In Martin's mind, Pennsylvania was a southern state.

The ever-increasing bickering and griping — the litany of the American soldier — must have warmed Washington's heart. His men no longer were content to suffer in silence; they were alive and complaining — loudly. The American fighting man was regaining his strength, his spirit and his will to live.

On 5 April, Washington and members of his staff rode four miles toward Philadelphia to greet General Charles Lee, formerly a prisoner of the British, and escort him through the pickets to Valley Forge. The exchanged prisoner was "entertained" by Mrs. Washington "with an Elegant Dinner, and the Music Playing the whole time." The next morning, Elias Boudinot wrote, Lee "lay very late and Breakfast was detained for him. When he came out he looked as dirty as if he had been in the Street all night. Soon after I discovered that he had brought a miserable dirty hussy with him from Philadelphia (a British Sergeant's wife) and had actually taken her into his Room by a Back Door and she had slept with him that night."

Though not a totally accepted practice, Lee had found yet another reason for living. So did other men in the camp at Valley Forge. Three Virginia girls made the trip north and married their soldier sweethearts, setting up house in the rough camp cabins. Other soldiers went on romantic excursions into the countryside, finding suitable mates among the local farm girl population.

The winter had taken its toll on some; it had strengthened others. Many who survived found they had greater reasons to live than ever before. They had wives, families and girlfriends. That was reason enough to continue. All that was left was for the British to leave Philadelphia and engage them once more on the field of battle.

I never realized as I wood-spooned caviar onto crackers that this delicacy, so tied to the Soviet Union, had played an important part in the turnaround of the

Continental Army. Having lived in states where the first run of the fish in the spring turns grown men into little boys, I can recall the fishermen of Grand Rapids, Michigan, running to the Grand River each spring to net basketsfull of smelt. Even now in Virginia, workmen will not schedule themselves to do anything in the early days of spring. Rather, they rush out to angle for the first catch. In many respects, they are honoring an old American tradition.

George Washington reviewing the troops at Valley Forge. Illustration by John Andrew was first published in Ballou's Pictorial, 13 September 1856.

Chapter Fourteen————

The Turning Point

Though Congress did not keep its commander-in-chief informed on its foreign relations efforts, George Washington was well aware of the measures being taken to bring France into the War for Independence on the American side.

But the general believed that any attempts at gaining French support would be fruitless. Washington considered the royal courts of Europe too full of intrigue and laxity to provide the colonists with anything more than "underhand assistance."

The winter was over and the warmth of April brought with it fresh gossip to Valley Forge that France would take the ultimate step and recognize the rebel government. On 30 April 1778, General Washington received two unofficial letters which said, as he summarized them, "that the court of France has recognized (the colonies) as free and independent states; that Britain is in greater ferment than she ever was since the Revolution, and that all Europe is getting into a flame . . . I believe no event was ever received with a more heartfelt joy."

The American commander was happy because the treaty of recognition also provided for a military alliance should France's actions get France into war with England. With England battling France,

British attention would be diverted and there would be fewer American lives sacrificed. At the same time, he was uncertain as to the accuracy of the reports. It was gossip, he told himself, nothing more. He needed confirmation and he wrote his superiors, the Congress, requesting official notice so that he could properly inform his troops.

By 5 May, he had heard nothing from Congress and so he issued routine orders for the day. When they were about to be sent to the unit commanders, a visitor brought a three-day old copy of the *Pennsylvania Gazette* to Washington's headquarters. The newspaper contained an entire section on the ramifications of the treaty! Congress might not have had time to tell its military commander, but it had sufficient time to get proper publicity.

To the previously-written orders, Washington appended the following:

"It having please the Almighty ruler of the Universe propitiously to defend the causes of the United American States and finally, by raising us up a powerful friend among the princes of the earth, to establish our liberty and Independence upon lasting foundations, it becomes us to set apart a day for gratefully acknowledging the divine goodness and celebrating the important event which we owe to his benign interposition."

Von Steuben had been successful in turning Washington's country bumpkins and clumsy clerks into an expert army. The baron wanted an opportunity to demonstrate the men's prowess and also to deflate his critics. History provided the proper moment. Washington scheduled the celebration for 9 a.m., 6 May. With his staff beside him, the commander-in-chief rode to the parade, where a clergyman read a summary of the treaty. So taken was he with the moment, the man of the cloth waxed eloquent for an hour-and-a-half. When he finally finished, the men were ordered back to their huts to collect their weapons and return to the ranks to participate in a martial extravaganza staged by von Steuben.

As Washington rode to a spot where he could review the entire operation, he could hear the commands, echoing through the fields with an unheard air of professionalism. Once in ranks, the men went through the preliminary motions that the Prussian had drilled into them. Inspectors goose-stepped through the ranks checking this, correcting that. Then there was silence.

A cannon was fired and the men moved forward . . . on command "the several brigades marched by their right," Henry Laurens wrote, "to their posts in order of battle." With frightening precision, they were shortly under the general's gaze. The Continental Army stood before their commander, glaring at an imaginary enemy . . . silent and motionless as the rock formations they passed on their march to the Forge the winter before. Washington stood silent — thinking back a few months when this same group of soldiers would have swayed before him, shifting from foot to foot, scratching their noses.

From the artillery park, the cannon began to report — 13 in all, fired one after another. When the last roar echoed through the valley, the men went into their *feu de joie*, the fire of joy. Excitement in the ranks mounted as each man fired his musket in turn. Down the first line and back across the next, the weapons sounded. Thousands of men waited . . . waited for that once-in-a-lifetime experience — to fire their muskets in the presence of their leader and the entire American Army.

Anxious to the last, von Steuben could not relax until he felt the firing was "executed to perfection." And it was. After the last man had pulled the trigger and the spark from the flint on frizzen ignited the black powder, the officers led the troops in a number of cheers: "Long Live the King of France! And Long Live the Friendly European Powers." and then, "To the American States." Thirteen cannon roared again. The frenzied excitement continued until the unit commanders ordered a repeat of the *feu de joie*. That's what the rank and file wanted. They wanted to be part of the celebration. Following the musket fire, the jubilant men were marched back through the smoke to their camps where extra rations of rum awaited them.

The pageant over, Washington cantered to a hastily-constructed amphitheater, built out of officers' tents, in front of the artillery park. There, he, his officers and visiting guests celebrated until dusk. The entertainment concluded with patriotic toasts . . . and then Washington took his leave. It was a joyous day.

Back in his own headquarters, the pleasure of the moment was replaced with warmer thoughts in the mind of George Washington. Since England might now be in another European war with France, there possibly might not be another campaign in America. The war, this brutal war, might end shortly.

That thought played on his mind. Quickly, he drafted a note to his stepson, countermanding previous instructions. This letter told the young man that he was not, under any circumstances, to sell any of Washington's acreage: "Lands are permanent," he wrote, "rising fast in value, and will be very dear when our independency is established and the importance of America better known."

Washington slept that night; his dreams filled with peace... peace and a return to his home at Mount Vernon. But, as it turned out, the war continued for another three years.

It occurred to me a long time ago that our leaders have the same fears and insecurities as do we. Ever since Watergate, I think Americans have looked at our leaders with less than an all-approving eye. This has not always been the case. George Washington, because he was our first president, has had to put up with a great deal of legend and myth. Sometimes it is difficult — and unpopular — to bring our leaders back to normal size. In 1983, I wrote a magazine article attacking the myth of Abraham Lincoln. The article drew a great deal of atten-tion, including a United Press International wire story that appeared all over the country. I was pretty happy to see my research reach such an audience, until I visited my local Italian deli and the clerk refused to wait on me because of what I wrote. But, it's the truth, I told her. Even so, she reponded, why did you have to write it? I am sure that this lady was — and is — not alone. We, as Americans, sometimes have a hard time accepting reality.

THE MESCHIANZA.

Major John Andre, architect
of The Meschianza.

A typical headdress worn by
a female guest from a sketch
by Major Andre.

The tickets were engraved
and, at the top, surrounded by
the motto "vive, vale!" is the
general's crest.

A view of the military procession.

Chapter Fifteen————

Howe's Farewell

Garrison duty can be boring, especially to the professional soldier whose appetite is whetted by the rattle of cannon, the clatter of sabers.

While Philadelphia did not have the allure of London or Paris, it was a most palatable place for garrison duty. And, as the winter of 1777-78 progressed, the British troops under Sir William Howe's command found their time taken up with eating, drinking and carousing.

A more disciplined man, a spit-and-polish commander, would have drilled and marched his men into lean, tough troops. But Sir William was content to relax in "London on the Delaware" with his Boston lady, Mrs. Joshua Loring. Besides, why should he do anything? He had made a request in November to be relieved of command. All he was doing was sitting fast, waiting for orders. Howe's lack of action in the colonies was the source of great criticism far and wide. One of his waggish critics, in fact, suggested that Howe be elevated to the peerage and given the title of "Lord Delay-war." In April of 1778, Sir William Howe's wait was over — he received word that he could go home.

Though his popularity was at an ebb in England, Howe retained the admiration and loyalty of his officers. For the most part, they were sorry to see him leave. To express their sentiments, Major John Andre, who would shortly suffer the ignominious death of a spy, conceived the idea of a party to celebrate the commander's departure. With carefully cultivated skills, Andre prepared a party to end all parties: The Meschianza.

The Meschianza. It is an Italian word which translates to a medley, a mixture of events. And The Meschianza was a most unusual blend. Andre's theme was medieval chivalry. For the site of his fete, he selected the beautiful "country" home of Quaker merchant Joseph Wharton. "Walnut Grove," located on what is now the south side of Washington Avenue, near Fourth Street, was ideal for Andre's plans. Its lush lawns extended from the mansion itself a full half mile to the banks of the Delaware River.

Monday, 18 May 1778, was picked as the date and ornately-embellished invitations were issued to every person of influence and affluence in Philadelphia. Howe's successor, General Henry Clinton, was invited — though he was embarrassed by the whole situation. So, too, were Lord Francis Rawdon, General Wilhelm von Knyphausen, and most of the city's beautiful young ladies . . . Tory and Whig alike.

Even 17-year-old Peggy Shippen, soon to be the wife of General Benedict Arnold, planned to attend. Some historians contend she didn't attend because her father, former Philadelphia Mayor Edward Shippen, intervened at the last minute and refused to let her go. Peggy's name, however, graces the guest list. Rebecca Franks, daughter of a wealthy Jewish merchant, also attended. Her father's firm had brought the Liberty Bell to Philadelphia in 1752.

On the afternoon of the 18th, a flotilla of British warships, merchantmen and transports sailed from Knight's Wharf on the Delaware. Divided into three groups, each had a galley for dignitaries, ten flat boats for other guests and a band. It was a splendid sight: Flags of other nations and states — including the American "Stars and Stripes" — stood at stiff attention in the breeze, garlands of flowers covered the galleys, and British seamen rowed in time to the music. Cannon from 300 British ships anchored in the harbor saluted the 400 guests as they stepped ashore at "Walnut Grove" and moved to the mansion, flanked by columns of grenadiers and a line of light horse cavalry.

To add excitement to his "meschianza," Andre had constructed a 450-square-foot jousting field in front of the house on which two teams of knights, bedecked in chivalrous regalia, waited on mounts to entertain the guests. One side, the "Knights of the Blended Rose," were dressed in red and white; the others, the "Knights of the Burning Mountain," in yellow and white.

One small boy couldn't perceive the difference between the two groups. Turning to him, a British officer said: "Why, child, the Knights of the Burning Bush are tomfools, and the Knights of the Blended Rose are damned fools. I know of no other difference between them."

The gauntlet was thrown down, the knights took their lances from pages and, "making a general salute to each other . . . dashed at each other with their spears, then on a second charge fired their pistols and finally engaged each other with their swords." No blood was shed in the mock battle and the ladies decided it should not continue, as tradition would have it, to the death.

Honor satisfied, the knights and their ladies, followed by the assemblage, marched through two triumphal arches. The first suggested a moral theme, honoring Admiral Richard Howe — Neptune smiling down on sailors with drawn cutlasses. The other arch celebrated the victories of the admiral's brother. At the summit stood a figure of Fame "and various military trophies."

After being suitably impressed by the contrived artworks, the knights and damsels entered the spacious hall, its panels painted by Captain Oliver DeLancey to resemble Siena marble.

The guests slaked their thirst with "tea, lemonade and other cooling liquor." Once satisfied, they proceeded to the ballroom, "decorated in a light, elegant style of painting . . . These decorations were heightened by 85 mirrors, decked with rose-pink silk ribbands and artificial flowers; and in the intermediate space were 34 branches with wax-lights."

Dancing continued until 10 p.m., when the windows of the ballroom were thrown open "and a magnificent bouquet of rockets began the fireworks." Twenty displays, each more spectacular than its predecessor, were arranged by chief engineer John Montresor. The climax was breathtaking: the triumphal arch "was illuminated amidst the uninterrupted flight of rockets and bursting of balloons. The military trophies on each side assumed a variety of transparent colours. The shell and flaming heart of the wings sent forth Chinese fountains, succeeded by fire-pots. Fame appeared at top, spangled with stars, and from her trumpet blowing the following device in letters of light, *Tes Lauriers son immortels* (Your laurels are immortal)."

Then John Andre read a poem he had composed for Howe:

Chained to our arms, while Howe the battle led,
Still round those files her wings shall Conquest spread.

Loved though he goes, the spirit still remains
That with him, bore us o'er these trembling pains.

And, so as not to slight his new commander, Andre added:

Nor fear but equal honors shall repay
Each hardy deed where Clinton leads the way

At midnight, dinner was served. Twenty-four "black slaves in oriental dresses, with silver collars and bracelets . . . bending to the ground as the General and Admiral approached the salon . . . a *coup d'oest* beyond description magnificent," one account read. Sumptuous foods were served, including 50 pounds of jellies, syllabub, cakes and sweetmeats. Almost everyone enjoyed the party . . . or so it seemed. There were, of course, some exceptions. Thomas Jones, a Tory historian of New York, suggested that "the exhibition of this 'triumphal Meschianza' will be handed down to posterity as one of the most ridiculous, undeserved, and unmerited triumphs ever performed. Had the General been properly rewarded for his conduct while Commander-in-Chief in American, an execution, and not a Meschianza, would have been the consequence."

And, though the invitation list seemed all-inclusive, there were a few notable exceptions . . . such as officers under Washington's command. Shortly after 4 a.m., they reminded the British hosts of the slight, with a series of explosions. The Meschianza's sponsors explained the noises away as a final salute from all those soldiers who remained on duty, foregoing the fun. But that wasn't the case.

Not wanting to be left out, Captain Allan McLane and a company of infantry, infiltrated the British lines and set fire to their abatis, which connected the northern line of defense. They attacked and exchanged fire with the English. It was only a minor skirmish but McLane's men left behind iron camp kettles, filled with combustibles and fitted with time fuses, as standing invitations to the British to come closer to Valley Forge . . . and party as soldiers should. The British didn't accept the invitation.

The house where The Meschianza was held no longer exists. It is quite ironic, I think, that the site of the Wharton Mansion is now a playground, a playground which serves one of Philadelphia's worst public housing complexes: Southwark Plaza.

The house in which Howe lived during the British occupation of Philadelphia, located on Market Street, between 5th and 6th streets, later became Washington's residence.

Chapter Sixteen———

Moving Day

For the second time in 19 months, the sidewalks of Philadelphia were littered with the personal debris of its residents. This time, however, the furniture, bedding, paintings, and other memorabilia were not the possessions of the natives. They were the owned or confiscated belongings of the British . . . waiting to be carted off to wharves on the Delaware. At long last, the British were leaving Philadelphia.

At Cooper's Creek, on the Jersey side of the river, the King's men had constructed redoubts to form a beachhead for the crossing of troops and supplies. More than 500 sailors from the royal fleet spent a full week ferrying the army's gear, wagons and 5,000 horses across the river. The field guns, on the other hand, were left in position until the very last minute — just in case.

At Valley Forge, George Washington learned of the possibility of Philadelphia's evacuation on 16 June 1778 — from the son of the Peace Commissioner's laundress — so much for the general's intelligence gathering network! The rumor was confirmed by Captain Allan McLane, the dashing cavalryman who had, with some measure of success, interrupted The Meschianza, the farewell party for Sir William Howe. McLane and his small detachment of horse soldiers scouted the outskirts of Philadelphia and saw firsthand the evidence: the British were indeed on the move.

Back in town, the British soldiers were ordered to draw four days' rations and store them in their haversacks. The wagons were also stocked, with 20 days' supplies. Sir Henry Clinton, the 48-year-old, paunchy, nearsighted and neurotic replacement for Howe, had received orders shortly after his arrival. "I cannot understand (the orders)," he said, "nor dare I disobey them. I am directed to evacuate Philadelphia. My fate is hard," he complained; "forced to an apparent retreat with such an army is mortifying." His destination was New York.

Though Clinton had criticized Howe's lack of action, he hated to see his predecessor leave, perhaps because he would be looked at and compared to him. On a public level, Clinton said he considered the brothers Howe an "irresistible" combination. Only they, he believed, could defeat the patriots. "I therefore cannot suppose it possible," he wrote, "that this command should fall upon my shoulders." But it had. And, as a good soldier, it was his duty to comply.

The route from Philadelphia to New York, decided upon by Clinton and his subordinate commanders, was through the generally hostile New Jersey countryside. They expected Washington to hover around their retreating flanks and attack at will. Unfortunately, Washington was not completely certain of their final destination or their route. During the night of 17 June, the British troops marched beyond Philadelphia's city limits and camped. At 3 the next morning they trooped to Gloucester Point where the fleet awaited them.

Not all the men made the exodus from Philadelphia. A good many German mercenaries and some British regulars, who had married local girls, decided to stay with their families. So, without much ado, they took advantage of the confusion . . . and deserted.

Henry Clinton spent the early morning hours of the 18th seated upon a rock at Gloucester Point . . . worrying, and expecting — at any second . . . to be assaulted by an American horde. But his anxiety was wasted. All was quiet, except for the grumblings of the sleepy soldiers and the crunch of wagon wheels on the ground. By 10 o'clock, every man and gun was across the Delaware and the British army marched five miles to Haddonfield, unmolested. There it remained for the next day.

As the Englishmen were regrouping in New Jersey, George Roberts wheeled his mount in front of Washington's headquarters at Valley Forge and, in the early morning light, gave the news that Philadelphia was free. And, as the last of His Majesty's soldiers stepped ashore, "Light-Horse Harry" Lee's cavalry galloped through the empty streets of Philadelphia down to the landing.

By nightfall, 18 June, Philadelphia was again in American hands. That evening, a watchman walked the streets, announcing that a curfew was in effect, by order of Colonel Daniel Morgan. The Philadelphia the Americans found was not the city they remembered in their dreams. The British had neglected sanitation and the city lacked natural drainage. "It stank so abominably," Henry Knox said, "that it was impossible to stay there."

For the most part, the buildings were in fair shape, one civilian noted, but "the morals of the inhabitants have suffered greatly." The young ladies of Philadelphia, he went on to say, were seriously afflicted with a strange disease, jokingly referred to as "scarlet fever," contracted during the long British occupation. "Many people," another exclaimed, "do not hesitate in supposing that most of the young ladies who were in the city with the enemy and wear the present fashionable dresses have purchased them at the expense of their virtue."

It was to this city, the City of Brotherly Love, that Congress returned 25 June . . . to continue the business of government in the colonial capital. Because the State House was "filthy and sordid," they set up offices in College Hall. It didn't really matter where they met after all. They had returned.

I found it amazing that Clinton was such a paranoid individual. As I look back on the situation, I find that many military officers are selected for command — not because they are such dynamic leaders but because they have the right backgrounds. It was for the British, and it is for the Americans.

Washington rallies the American troops at Monmouth, after General Charles Lee decided the Americans could not win in a direct confrontation with the British.

Chapter Seventeen ———

An "Elusive" Finale

With white cockades in their hats and "Yankee Doodle" on their lips, more than 13,000 members of the Continental Army crossed the Delaware River at Coryell's Ferry, from New Hope, Pennsylvania, to Lambertville, New Jersey. The sun was high and temperatures soared past the 90 degree mark on 23 June 1778; but the American Army, the best armed, disciplined, equipped and fed troops Washington had ever fielded, was on the move.

If the war was ever going to end, there was going to have to be a beginning. So, when Washington met with his generals at Hopewell on the 24th, he looked for advice as to an active or passive campaign strategy. Nathanael Greene, von Steuben, Louis LeBeque de Presle Duportail, Anthony Wayne, and the Marquis de Lafayette wanted to go on the offensive. The only major opposition was from Major General Charles Lee, and subscribed to by William "Lord Stirling" Alexander and the bookseller, Henry Knox. Ever since he had returned from royal imprisonment to friendly quarters, Lee had been extremely critical of Washington, the strength of his troops and the miracle wrought by von Steuben. Though he was quite vocal, very few people listened to him.

This time, however, Washington did . . . for awhile. The commanders agreed to avoid a general engagement, but to send a force of 1,500 men to "act as occasion may serve, on the enemy's left flank and rear." A few hours after the meeting, new intelligence was received: the British were moving from Allentown to Monmouth Court House [now Freehold, N.J.]. This called for a revision of Washington's plans. He decided to send troops under General Daniel Morgan to harass the other side of the British column. Washington himself led the main body to Kingston, with an advance guard of 4,000 men under Lafayette at Cranbury.

The born-again Continental Army shadowed Sir Henry Clinton and his army for several days. The British march was slowed greatly by fear of attack — Clinton's paranoia had intensified, and hampered by the excess baggage and carriages of Loyalists fleeing Philadelphia. Washington's men marched parallel to the retreating foe, and about 30 miles to the north. They clung to the British flanks, bothering them like the fiery mosquitoes endemic to New Jersey. On 25 June, Washington recognized that Clinton was veering toward Sandy Hook on the Atlantic coast, where English ships could rescue him. At this point, the commander-in-chief decided he was ready: he would fight Clinton and, this time, win.

The plan was simple. Lafayette would attack the British the next day and occupy them in a delaying action. This would provide time for Washington to bring up the main body and defeat the British. It was all very simple . . . until General Lee imposed himself. Though he had initially refused command, Lee changed his mind when he realized the size of the colonial force and the opportunity to be the hero. Besides, he felt it "would have an odd appearance" if he didn't take command. Rather than precipitate a division in the command cadre, Lafayette told Washington he would be willing to relinquish the honor and serve under Lee.

On 27 June, Lieutenant Colonel Alexander Hamilton reduced to paper Washington's oral instructions to Lee: attack and hold until the main army could arrive. Lee was also instructed to call his brigadiers and "concert some mode of attack." Lee arranged a meeting for 5:30 that night . . . but didn't show up. When asked about his absence, he shrugged it off, saying he didn't have any orders to communicate. The entire affair began to assume strange overtones.

Unaware of the American intrigue, the British arrived at Monmouth Court House, made camp and prepared themselves for offense, defense, or a good night's sleep.

Lee's troops moved against the British rear on the morning of 28 June. Though von Knyphausen's Hessians and two British brigades had departed at 4 o'clock in the morning, the Americans didn't advance until 9:30 due to delayed and contradictory orders. Lee's men crossed the rugged terrain and three ravines to reach the enemy's column. Lee had still not communicated an organized battle plan to his subordinates. They would have to play the battle by ear.

The rank and file were ready. Private Joseph Plumb Martin's captain told his men: "You have been wanting to fight — now you shall have fight enough before the night." But, Lee apparently had lost his fighting edge while a prisoner of the British. When he realized his troops were outnumbered three to two, Lee ordered his men to retreat across the ravines. "One order succeeded another," John Laurens stated, "with a rapidity and indecision calculated to ruin us... All this disgraceful retreating," he said in disgust, "passed without the firing of a musket over ground which might have been disputed inch by inch."

Clinton toyed with Lee. He didn't want a full-scale battle. He wanted time for his baggage trains to slip by; that was all. Anthony Wayne, despite the odds and always the optimist, saw a good chance for success. He, above all, remembered Germantown. Lafayette urged Lee to press forward. "You do not know British soldiers," Lee replied, "we cannot stand against them." A few minutes after that conversation, the startled Frenchman received orders to withdraw. He could see his men falling back already. Apparently Lee had instructed some of his brigades to "take your men any place where they will be safe."

Along the march, Washington listened to the rumble of cannon and leaned forward in his saddle to catch the rattle of small arms fire. It was noon and he was puzzled by the silence as he approached the battle scene. Fleeing infantrymen told him they were retreating. "Even rout," Hamilton remembered, "would not be too strong a word." According to von Steuben, the enlisted men were furious at the "senseless" retreat. But not so much as Washington. When the commander-in-chief met Lee on the field, his latent violent temper erupted. At his later court-martial, Lee remembered being told: "I desire to know, sir, what is the reason, when arises this disorder and confusion?" Several eyewitnesses depicted the confrontation in saltier terms.

After meeting Washington and reminding him that the whole affair "was contrary to his opinion, that he was averse to an attack, or general engagement, and was against it in council — that while the enemy were so superior in cavalry we could not oppose them," Lee moved to the rear. On the way back, he ran into von Steuben, who was advancing his men. Wondering where the German was going, he was told the British were retreating in confusion. Not so, Lee replied, "they are only resting themselves . . . I am sure there is some misunderstanding in your being (sent) to advance with these troops."

Blinded by rage, Washington spurred his mount forward and took command himself. He quickly turned the troops back into the face of the enemy. With Greene on the right, Alexander on the left, and Washington in the center, the determined Continentals stopped four fierce British assaults. The men, following Washington's example, fought with renewed fury, despite the heat of the day which was "almost too hot to live in."

Whatever errors and mistakes Washington had made in the past disappeared as he led his men into the Battle of Monmouth Court House. His presence gave heart to the common soldiers; his decisiveness, new resolve to his officers.

As the Continentals reengaged the British, the legend of Molly Pitcher began: a young woman who had been supplying water to the overheated soldiers dropped her bucket and manned a cannon when her husband fell.

The Redcoats held their ground until their 80-cartridge-per-man supply ran out. Clinton sent a courier to von Knyphausen to bring up reinforcements. By 5 p.m., the British leader ordered a withdrawal along the entire line. The troops who had been trained by von Steuben and seasoned by the Valley Forge winter tasted blood, and they savored it. The American officers "had to force (the troops) to retreat," Private Martin said, "so eager were they to be revenged on the invaders of their country and rights . . . grating as this order was to their feelings, we were obliged to comply." To prevent Clinton from attacking his position, Washington located fresh infantry and artillery on the high hills.

But no new attack came. Both armies were exhausted. Half of all the British dead were attributed to death by sunstroke. Many of the horses died in their tracks, including Washington's white charger, a gift from New Jersey's Governor William Livingston. By nightfall, the Continental Army possessed the field. Washington intended to resume the attack at dawn and force Clinton to surrender. But that was not to be. While Washington and Lafayette lay on their cloaks discussing Lee's erratic behavior, the British stole into the night and escaped. Two days later they reached Sandy Hook, arriving in New York on 5 July.

Though the American fighting men had shown great valor and discipline in battle, complete victory had escaped them again. Both sides claimed a win; the British, because they reached their goal, New

York; the Americans, because they possessed the field of battle and counted 2,000 British deserters.

The Battle of Monmouth Court House was the last major engagement in the North . . . and the longest of the entire war. If it had not been for Lee's incompetence and indecision, the Continental Army could have duplicated the victory at Saratoga and ended the war in the cornfields of New Jersey.

One can only sense the frustration of George Washington at Monmouth Court House. Here he had the British in the palm of his hand, and his fellow-Virginian, General Lee, loses his courage at the crucial moment. A lesser man, perhaps, would have drawn his sidearm and disciplined Lee. But, Washington was never a lesser man.

Mary Ludwig Hays, the real-life person behind the legendary Molly Pitcher.

Chapter Eighteen ─────

Doing a Man's Job

She was a woman of little education, Private Joseph Plumb Martin remembered; she smoked, chewed tobacco and swore like a trooper. Other veterans of the American Revolution recalled her as "rather stout and red" and "a coarse and uncouth looking female." Perhaps she was, but she was Molly Pitcher, and legendary people often have critics.

Some historians feel no clear-cut evidence exists that Molly was *one* individual; they contend she is the embodiment of several historic ladies. But there *was* a real-life Molly Pitcher. Tradition, though, has so embroidered her image that it's almost impossible to separate fact from fantasy.

"Molly Pitcher" was with her husband's regiment when the Americans faced the British at Monmouth Court House 28 June 1778. The day was very hot with the mercury rising over the 100 degree mark and men falling to the ground, many dying of heat prostration. Since the men needed water to lubricate their swollen tongues, it seemed logical that a non-combatant would come forward and bring them water. Molly, as the stories go, exposed herself to constant British fire. Hand-me-down tales have her rescuing and nursing wounded soldiers, and, when her husband fell, she took charge of his cannon and carried on until the battle's end.

In a series of ten papers on the life of this legendary lady, five state her husband was "wounded at Monmouth"; three that he was "killed." The other two decided he was "mortally wounded" or "died from the heat." Legend also has it that Molly spent the next seven years in the army; that she was commissioned by George Washington on the spot and recommended for half-pay for life; that she is buried in potter's field in Pennsylvania, and on the banks of the Hudson.

But the real-life Molly Pitcher was, in many respects, more interesting than the fanciful tales.

Mary Ludwig was born 13 October 1754 in a small settlement in Mercer County, New Jersey, a few miles from Trenton. Her father, John George Ludwig, had emigrated from the German Palatinate. In the rural community, Mary — affectionately called "Molly" — lived with her family until Dr. William Irvine's wife came to Trenton and noticed the young girl. Without much ado, Mrs. Irvine hired Molly Ludwig as a domestic and took her home to Carlisle, Pennsylvania.

The year was 1769 and the young woman was a fine employee. But something other than her dusting and polishing caught the eye of the town barber, young John Casper Hays. After what must have been a whirlwind courtship, Hays married the 15-year-old Molly on 24 July 1769. Both continued working at their independent jobs, perhaps with an idea of saving enough money to buy a farm of their own. But that was not to be.

War was in the air. Carlisle was an important rendezvous during the Revolution, and it had been a military post for many years. It was also a cauldron of patriotism. When the rumors of war became reality, Molly's husband and her employer enlisted to defend their land and their country. John Hays joined Proctor's 1st Pennsylvania Artillery as a gunner on 1 December 1775. When his term expired, he reenlisted, this time in the 7th Pennsylvania Regiment, commanded by Captain John Alexander, of Carlisle. Irvine entered the field in 1776, as a colonel of the 7th Pennsylvania. Captured at Three Rivers, Irvine remained a prisoner on parole until he was exchanged on 21 April 1778. Once free, he returned to his old unit, where John Casper Hays was a private. He arrived in time for the battle of Monmouth.

While the men were off to war, Molly Hays continued to work for Mrs. Irvine. After Washington and his troops left Valley Forge and regained Philadelphia, her family — still in New Jersey — sent a messenger to Carlisle, inviting their daughter to come visit. The courier also brought a note from John, who wanted her at his side. Letting her heart lead the way, Molly Hays set out on horseback; she would once again be with her family . . . and her husband.

The events of the war and Molly's life came together at Monmouth. As the battle raged, Molly — who apparently stayed with her man — carried water from a neighboring spring to the parched soldiers. Possibly she carried the water in a cannoneer's bucket, rather than a pitcher. Whatever vessel she carried, she was indeed a welcome sight.

Late in the afternoon, she approached her husband's unit. As the smoke cleared, she spotted a soldier lying beside the gun. Her heart stopped. She thought it was John! But after a closer look, she found it was one of his comrades; John was only wounded. Without thinking of her own safety, she took his place . . . but for how long? No one knows.

Some legends have her commanding the artillery crew. Based on contemporary evidence, however, she probably took her husband's place as the ammunition runner, passing the 6-pound shells from supply to cannon. Interestingly, that task is usually performed by extremely strong men because the strenuous work requires strength and stamina.

"While in reaching (for) a cartridge," Private Martin recalled, "and having one of her feet as far before the other as she could step, a cannon shot from the enemy passed directly between her legs without doing any damage (other) than carrying away the lower part of her petticoat. Looking at it with apparent concern," he noted, "she observed that it was lucky it did not pass a little higher, for in that case it might have carried away something else, and continued her occupation."

The common soldiers were astonished by her bravery and called her "sergeant" and "Major Molly." There is no record that she stayed with the army after the encounter. She did, however, cook and wash for the soldiers at Carlisle Barracks following the war. In her later years, she kept a store at the southeastern part of town, not far from the house where Major John Andre and Lieutenant John Despard were confined after their surrender at St. Johns in 1775.

Shortly after the war, John Casper Hays died, leaving Molly with nothing but a son [he served as an infantry sergeant during the War of 1812]. After John's death, Molly married another soldier, a friend of her late husband, George McKolly [also spelled McAuley, McCauley, McCauly]. Because she could not tolerate his shiftlessness, Molly left McKolly and supported herself as a laundress and nursemaid.

During her waning years, Mary Ludwig Hays McKolly was just like the other old soldiers of the Revolution. She liked to smoke her pipe, chew tobacco, drink and curse like the rest.

Mrs. Barbara Park of Carlisle, who died in 1896, knew Molly well. On 8 September 1826, Barbara and her brother were rushing to the cornerstone ceremony at the Episcopal Church. In their childish haste, they slipped into the stone quarry on the public square. The first person to climb down the embankment to rescue them was Mrs. McKolly. "This is nothing but a flea bite," she told the children, "to what I have seen." Other evidence exists that, despite her homely appearance and lack of education, Molly McKolly was always willing to pitch in and do a kind act.

On 14 February 1822 — coincidentally Valentine's Day — the Clerk of the Senate of Pennsylvania introduced Bill No. 265: "An Act for the relief of Molly McKolly, widow of a soldier . . . " A week later, after committee discussion, the bill was amended to cite her "for services rendered" in the war. The annuity specified — $40 "semi-yearly during life from January 1, 1822" — was for her personal services, not those of her husband. In fact, the law providing pensions to widows was not approved until 4 July 1836, four years after the real Molly Pitcher died in a small stone house near the southeast corner of Bedford and North Streets in Carlisle.

To remember her deeds, a committee arranged for a monument in Mrs. McKolly's honor as part of the American Centennial. Spearheaded by Peter Spahr of Carlisle, the monument was unveiled 4 July 1876.

Molly Pitcher has taken a great deal of criticism over the years. Jealous, chauvinistic men have called her a campfollower and worse. The legendary Molly Pitcher might have been offended. But Mary Ludwig Hays McKolly would have sat on her porch, puffed on her pipe, and smiled. She didn't have to prove anything; she was secure in her own accomplishments. As a contemporary poet wrote:

> Oh, Molly, Molly, here's to you!
> Sweet Honor's roll with aye be richer,
> To hole the name of Molly Pitcher.

It seems that the heroines of the Revolution have come under more criticism than the men. Schoolchildren still hear that George Washington couldn't tell a lie, that he threw a silver dollar across the Potomac, and that he chopped down the cherry tree. Though those stories have been proved false, creations of the legend-making Parson Weems. But, we have a great deal of proof that Molly Pitcher existed and did what she is reported to have done . . . and we have a good idea that Lydia Darragh passed messages to Washington. When are we going to come of age and provide equal credit to women?

The American Fighting Men, 1777-78.

Chapter Nineteen————

To Die For One's Country

The men who fought in George Washington's army were unlike the men who fought in World War II, Korea, or Vietnam. In fact, they were unlike any army this nation has ever mustered. Why? Because they had no precedent, there was nothing with which to draw comparisons. As a result, why they were willing to fight and die becomes important to anyone studying the military history of this country.

Life is man's only mortal possession. It is the vehicle by which he transforms his dreams to fulfillment, and feels the wonder of what he has done. Life is everything, for death remains the ultimate mystery to the living.

What, then, can man consider to be more important than life itself?

What makes a man give his life?

Since the beginning of time men have made the ultimate sacrifice for causes and ideals which they consider greater than God's gift to them.

Most often in wars. Often for freedom.

So it was with the men who served under George Washington. They fought the bitter cold, the superior British forces, and the fear of death with a resolution born of free men.

Men in the flower of youth and the shadow of age perished under the rain of lead and fire.

These men were not the smartly-uniformed, well-armed, brilliantly-trained soldiers of the grand English and European style. Nor were they mercenaries, the lifelong soldiers of fortune skilled as the hawk, lusting for the bounty.

The soldiers who fought for American Independence were ordinary human beings...workers...farmers...taxpayers...but more. They were infused with a spirit of their time...a spirit that harnessed their sense of duty, and demanded the extraordinary in the name of Liberty for their country.

America was their land. Their War of Independence was not a European war fought to perpetuate old ideas and institutions. It was the classic life and death struggle for a free society. If the American cause were to perish, each and every American would perish — for they would no longer be able to walk as free men. They would crawl under the thumb of tyranny.

It is not easy to sacrifice everything. Neither is it easy for a man to risk death — even under the banner of his beliefs. But these men did that. They believed in Justice, Equality and Freedom. They believed in these intangibles not so much as philosophical points of discussion but as a way of life. They believed with such fervor they were willing to do battle — and die — in defense of them.

Many had lived under oppression in their native lands. Many had come to the colonies to begin life anew...independent...free from the past. But the old restraints and pressures appeared in the new land.

A man tastes freedom. It is the warmth of spring. Once savored, it is desired forever. This is what spurred the American fighting man onward.

These were men who espoused the "cause of liberty" for their own political and economic benefits. A man is a man...he has strength, but he also has shortcomings. But, the true Cause of Liberty dominated the American dream.

The War for Independence was a struggle "where the Object is neither Glory nor extent of territory, but a Defense of all that is dear and valuable in Life," as George Washington once wrote. A colonist could look at his young son and envision a dim future for the boy under the restraints of foreign oppression. He could see his son a young man...and his earnings constantly eroded by unfair and indiscriminate taxes...or the young man perhaps shunted off to fight his oppressor's battles, at the whim of the absentee monarch. The American fighting man looked at the present and into the future — and his determination for freedom grew. He did not want his children and his children's children brought up in an atmosphere of fear and degradation. He wanted them to have the opportunity to earn all the things he did not have . . . but always wanted. It was for this he was willing to fight . . . and die.

The fledgling colonies were a beginning for some men . . . a last chance for others. If they did not stand up to the unbearable taxation and the total lack of representation, they would perish . . . not only as a nation . . . but as men.

For this, they were willing to die.

Death is not easy. Man doesn't want to die and grasps at life's very last flicker. We are sure there were men who did not think they were going to die at Brandywine, Germantown, the forts on the Delaware, Monmouth Court House, or elsewhere. But they were ready to make that sacrifice for a free nation.

Many died during the War for Independence. We're sure that most did not consider themselves heroes. They were just men who believed in the justice of their cause . . . the cause encompassed in the declaration that "all men are created equal." They believed all men should be allowed to practice this equality without fear. To suffer . . . even to die . . . for something one believes only reinforces that belief.

There were few cowards in Washington's army . . . only frightened men and boys with ideals. They were frightened because they were facing overwhelming odds . . . and death. They didn't understand death. All they knew was life. Yet, if they did not fight for their beliefs, there would be no life for them . . . or for their families . . . or their friends.

They sacrificed their lives for all mankind. They did not flinch at making this sacrifice. They died so that future generations might live in freedom. Today we live in a free land because of their sacrifice.

The world in which we live is far from perfect. Its faults are as numerous as the crevices in the earth. We are vocal and outspoken in our demands for change. America's fighting men fought and died so we would have the opportunity to be so vocal . . . and to make our world better. It is their greatest legacy.

On Memorial Day 1971, I stood before a group of several hundred people at Old Fort Mifflin and read the preceding document. Beginning in 1967 and continuing until 1976, I made an annual Memorial Day speech. This particular one was important to me. One of the young men who had become active in our restoration work as a teenager had joined the Army and gone off to Vietnam. I learned from his parents that he had been killed shortly before Memorial Day. As my thoughts of this youngster came into focus, the world I wanted to share with that audience came together.

Chapter Twenty ————

The Afterword

Why must
I die
in this
barren
place...
away
from men
I call
my friends?

Why can't
I live
and love
in peace
like men
throughout
the world?
Why must
I die?

Perhaps
I do
because
I must
if I
shall see
others,
my friends,
live free.

Throughout the years that I spent researching this period, I kept thinking about the rank-and-file, the men who rushed into battle knowing that they might not come out of combat alive. I also thought of this situation in contemporary terms. Was this a question that men asked themselves? Was this their answer?

Acknowledgments

It goes without saying that a number of people assisted me in the development of this book. Doug Bedell, who was the editorial page director at the *Bulletin*, was interested enough in my project to let it run on his editorial pages. Without his help, people might not have known what happened in Philadelphia after the signing of the Declaration of Independence.

My interest in this period began with my involvement, as president of the nonprofit Shackamaxon Society, in the restoration of Old Fort Mifflin. To answer questions of tourists and volunteers about the Revolution and the fort required me to spend many hours in archives and libraries. And, there were the people at Old Fort Mifflin who spurred me on when I was ready to drop; people like Harry J. Solimeo, who is as close to me as any blood relative. Harry served as treasurer of our organization and as my priestly confessor. I can't ignore Bill and Sandy Myers who believed, and the countless others who volunteered at the fort. Thanks are also in order to former Philadelphia Mayor James H. J. Tate and former Recreation Commissioner Bob Crawford who permitted me and the Society to create some living history.

Dale Floyd and Mike Musick at the National Archives were, as always, helpful. Dale has moved onwards and upwards in his career, and Mike gets mentioned in most books that use original material. John Platt from the Historical Society of Pennsylvania was always ready and able to pull out something that I needed at a moment's notice. Jerry Post, who at the time was the Free Library of Philadelphia's map collection maven, was exceptionally helpful.

I couldn't complete this set of acknowledgments without thanking Peter and Amy Alotta, my son and daughter. They grew up learning about Philadelphia and Revolutionary War history. Neither has lost the love for the subject. There are times when I question my involvements and wonder if I spent too much time helping to preserve the past and not enough time with my children. But, as my wife reminds me, they were at my side each and every minute at Fort Mifflin. It would have been different, she says, if I was a golfer.

121

There are others, too numerous to mention, who gave me a smile or a shove — when I needed one. To those nameless ones, I apologize.

Bibliography

Barton, George. *Little Journeys Around Old Philadelphia.* Philadelphia: The Peter Reilly Company, 1925.

————. *Walks and Talks About Old Philadelphia.* Philadelphia: The Peter Reilly Company, 1928.

Berg, Fred Anderson. *Encyclopedia of Continental Army Units.* Harrisburg, Pennsylvania: Stackpole Books, 1972.

Bill, Alfred Hoyt. *New Jersey and the Revolutionary War.* Princeton, New Jersey: D. Van Nostrand Co., Inc., 1964.

Boatner, Mark M. III. *Encyclopedia of the American Revolution.* New York: David McKay Co., Inc., 1966.

Bolton, Charles Knowles. *The Private Soldier Under Washington.* Port Washington, New York: Kennikat Press, Inc., 1964.

Brandt, Francis B., and Henry V. Gunmere. *Byways and Boulevards In and About Historic Philadelphia.* Philadelphia: privately published by the Corn Exchange National Bank, 1925.

Carrington, Henry B. *Battles of the American Revolution, 1775-1781.* New York: A. S. Barnes & Co., 1888.

Casey, William J. *Where & How the War Was Fought: An Armchair Tour of the American Revolution.* New York: William Morrow & Company, 1976.

Chronicles of the American Revolution. Alden T. Vaughan, ed. New York: Grosset & Dunlap, 1965.

Collins, Herman, and Wifred Jordan. *Philadelphia: A Story of Progress.* [4 vols.] Philadelphia: Lewis Historical Publishing Co., 1941.

Defences of Philadelphia in 1777. Worthington Chauncey Ford, ed. New York: De Capo Press, 1971.

Dictionary of Philadelphia. Philadelphia: privately published by John Wanamaker, 1887.

Eberlein, Harold, and Horace M. Lippincott. *The Colonial Homes of Philadelphia and Its Neighborhood.* Philadelphia: J. B. Lippincott Co., 1912.

Faris, John T. *Old Roads Out of Philadelphia.* Philadelphia: J. B. Lippincott Co., 1917.

Fisher, Sydney George. *The True Story of the American Revolution.* Philadelphia: J. B. Lippincott Co., 1912.

Fiske, John. *The American Revolution.* [2 vols.] Boston: Hougton Mifflin & Co., 1901.

Flexner, James Thomas. *George Washington: In the American Revolution, 1775-1783.* Boston: Little, Brown & Co., 1967.

Hagner, Charles V. *Early History of the Falls of Schuylkill, Manayunk, etc.* Philadelphia: Claxton, Remsen and Haffelfinger, 1869,

Hawk, David Freemen. *Paine.* New York: Harper & Row, 1974.

Heitman, Francis B. *Historical Register of Officers of the Continental Army.* Baltimore, Geneological Publishing Co., 1967.

Higginbotham. *The War of American Independence, Military Attitudes, Policies and Practices, 1763-1789.* New York: The Macmillan Co., 1971.

"Historic American Building Survey — Old Fort Mifflin," unpublished manuscript, 1969.

Hotchkin, Rev. S. F. *Ancient & Modern Germantown, Mount Airy and Chestnut Hill.* Philadelphia: P. F. Ziegler & Co., 1889.

Jackson, John W. *The Pennsylvania Navy, 1775-1781.* New Brunswick, New Jersey: Rutgers University Press, 1974.

Jackson, Joseph. *Encyclopedia of Philadelphia.* Harrisburg: The National Historical Association, 1931.

Kaplan, Lawrence S. *Colonies Into Nation: American Diplomacy 1763-1801.* New York: The Macmillan Co., 1972.

Leake, Isaac Q. *Memoir of the Life and Times of General John Lamb.* Albany, New York: Joel Munsel, 1850.

Lossing, B. J. *The Pictorial Field Book of the Revolution.* New York: Harper Brothers, 1852.

Luvaas, Jay. "Washington's Drillmaster," *American History Illustrated.* April 1967.

Makers of Philadelphia. Charles Morris, ed. Philadelphia: L. R. Hamersly & Co., 1894.

Martin, Joseph Plumb. *Private Yankee Doodle.* George F. Scheer, ed., Boston: Little, Brown & Co., 1962.

Miers, Earl Schenck. *Crossroads of Freedom.* New Brunswick. New Jersey: Rutgers University Press, 1971.

Montross, Lynn. *Rag, Tag and Bobtail: The Story of the Continental Army, 1775-1783.* New York: Harper & Brothers, 1952.

Moore, Frank. *Diary of the American Revolution.* London: Charles Scribner's, 1860.

Pennsylvania 1776. Robert Secor, John M. Pickering, and Irwin Richman, eds. University Park: The Pennsylvania State University Press, 1975.

A Rhode Island Chaplain in the Revolution [Letters of Ebenezer David to Nicholas Brown, 1775-1778]. Jeannette D. Black and William Greene Roehler, eds. Providence: The Rhode Island Society of the Cincinnati, 1949.

Rilling, Joseph R. *Baron Von Steuben and His Regulations.* Philadelphia: Ray Riling Arms Books Co., 1966.

Scharf, J. Thomas, and Thompson Wescott. *History of Philadelphia 1609-1884.* [4 vols.] Philadelphia: L. H. Evarts & Co., 1884.

Shackleton, Robert. *The Book of Philadelphia.* Philadelphia: Penn Publishing Company, 1926.

Smith, Samuel Stelle. *Fight for the Delaware 1777.* Monmouth Beach, New Jersey: Philip Freneau Press, 1970.

Stevens, S. K. *The Brandywine Battlefield Story.* Chadds Ford, Pennsylvania: Brandywine Battlefield Commission, undated.

Thompson, Ray. *Washington at Germantown.* Fort Washington, Pennsylvania: Bicentennial Press, 1975.

————. *Washington at Whitemarsh: Prelude to Valley Forge.* Fort Washington, Pennsylvania: Bicentennial Press, 1968.

Watson, John F. *Annals of Philadelphia, and Pennsylvania in the Olden Times.* [3 vols., revisions in vol. 3 by Willis P. Hazard] Philadelphia: Edwin S. Stuart, 1905.

Weigley, Russell F. *History of the United States Army.* New York: The Macmillan Co., 1967.

Wood, Gordon S. *The Creation of the American Republic 1776-1787.* Chapel Hill: University of North Carolina Press, 1969.

The Writings of George Washington. Worthington Chauncey Ford, ed. Vol. VI, 1777-78. New York: G. P. Putnam's Press, 1890.

"Thoughts on History and The Historian's Role"

History is the fabric of the world. As history pertains to the United States; it is what we are. Americans have set precedents which altered the way future generations live and behave . . . not only in this country but throughout the world. Think of the Declaration of Independence. Think of the U.S. Constitution. Think of the Atomic Bomb. Think of Vietnam. Think of any number of earth-shattering events.

We as a people have made history. And there are some of us who study it to gain an insight into ourselves and our fellowman. But what is history?

Basically history is the acts, ideas or events which shape the course of the future. A historian is a person who chronicles all this material and puts it into some semblance of order so future generations can profit from the mistakes their forebears made.

Each individual historian has carved our his own little niche — his own little area of expertise. Yet few take the time to sit down and explain what they consider to be their unique role in recounting history. Perhaps they haven't, because for some time history has been stigmatized by boring writing. Many consider the history books which were forced on them in school as nothing more than monotonous repetitions of dates and events. Few historical writings to which they were exposed provided the nonprofessional reader with an insight into the why — the explanation of the human involvement in making things happen the way they did.

History, after all, is the day-to-day diary of mankind. It does not exist because of any particular battle, treaty or event. It is created by man, and the teaching or writing of history should always reflect this fact. Written history must be alive for no other reasons than because it deals with life — and the lessons learned from living.

Ideal history should recreate the past as it actually was, complete with the smiles and sneers; the dimples and the warts. Too often the course of history has been altered because some monarch rose from his chambers with a headache, or because someone failed to read a particularly important message, or because another individual had an innate bias toward someone or something. In many instances, these examples of the shortcomings of human nature are more important to overall understanding than the final result itself and should be included. Unfortunately, objectivity is sometimes lost because most histories are written from the victor's point of view.

Because of man's makeup — and we cannot underscore the people-orientation of history too strongly — the study of the past must represent an amalgam of philosophy, psychology, science, and art. To narrate the story truthfully, the historian must practice those disciplines and add to them, functioning both as a detective and novelist. If he does not wear all these hats, his writing will read like a statistical compilation of births and deaths.

To begin, a historian must know what happened and then determine why it did. Though he cannot achieve absolute truth in his study, the historian can come closer to it than those who actually lived in the time gone by ... simply because the historian lacks personal involvement. To underscore that point ... Brigadier General Edwin H. Simmons, USMC (Ret.), told a group of my students that a true history of the Vietnam War could not be written until all the participants were dead.

Since the historian is remote from the events which he chronicles, his judgement will not harm him or others. At the same time, however, this detachment can also be detrimental. It is possible for the historian to tint his historical thinking with the popular views and myths of modern day. As an example, the writings on slavery written during the Sixties reflected the mood of the civil rights movement, while works on the same subject written in the Twenties and Thirties reflected the mood of an entirely different time period.

Why does someone write history? Simply so future men and women will know what we did before they arrived. Besides there is a vicarious pleasure in reliving the past. A history-writing author can play Walter Mitty and act out the lives of as many glamorous leaders from as many golden ages as he wants. He can also touch the genius of the past and revel in the adventure. Many of us today are too old or too out of shape to walk on the moon, but those of us who write history, we can be pioneers in another form of discovery.

Regardless of the difficulty in piecing together the jigsaw puzzle of the ages, writing history can be most pleasurable. And, to be entirely satisfying, history must be shared. So, reading it should elicit enjoyment in the reader's mind.

At all times and in all places, the historian must keep sight of his role as a minister to the past, the present and the future. By serving all three, he can perform an almost spiritual act — he exposes the ultimate questions of human existence and prepares future generations so they can eliminate the pitfalls and pratfalls to which their ancestors fell prey.

What I have attempted to create here is not a "history book." Rather I have tried to write an entertaining account of what transpired in the Delaware Valley area the year following the signing of the Declaration of Independence. I have tried not to burden the reader with foot- or endnotes, and have kept the accounts brief and to the point. Perhaps readers will have their curiosity peaked and will wish to delve deeper. I hope you do.

Robert I. Alotta, Ph.D.
Harrisonburg, Va., 1989

Index

130